Engraving and Enamelling

The art of champlevé

Engraving and Enamelling

The art of champlevé

Phil Barnes

CROWOOD

First published in 2019 by
The Crowood Press Ltd
Ramsbury, Marlborough
Wiltshire SN8 2HR

www.crowood.com

British Library Cataloguing-in-Publication Data
A catalogue record for this book is available from the British Library.

ISBN 978 1 78500 545 9

Disclaimer
This book and the information given is a record of my working practice. Many of the techniques used in enamelling and engraving involve hazardous materials, machinery and procedures. If all health and safety instructions are adhered to and given the respect they deserve, no problems should arise. The author and publisher accept no liability for any accidents howsoever caused to any reader following instructions from the text of this book.

Frontispiece: Abstract design No.1: silver engraved and enamelled vase by Phil Barnes. 130mm high and 90mm at the widest point.

Acknowledgements
I would like to acknowledge and thank all the people who have helped with the creation of this book, in particular those who have given images for it: Mr David Bainbridge of Milton Bridge Enamels, Elizabeth Gage Ltd, De Vroomen Design, Roger Doyle, Ingo Henn, The Ashmolean Museum Oxford and the V&A Museum London.

An even bigger thanks goes to my wife Linda for her support and encouragement, my ever on-hand 'sounding board', and above all for her photography skills that created the workshop images.

Graphic design and typesetting by Peggy & Co. Design Inc.
Printed and bound in Malaysia by Times Offset (M) Sdn Bhd

Contents

Preface

My working life began in 1967 at the age of fifteen, and 2017 marked a milestone for me of fifty years as a full-time professional enameller. During this time I trained three apprentices, ran workshops, and taught and lectured both in the UK and abroad. The passing on of knowledge is important, and to leave a written record of my way of working had always been an ambition.

I have a small book on enamelling, published back in 1927 by the French enameller Louis-Elie Millenet, which has been in my workshop for many years. This simple book, written by a professional, covers everything a book on enamelling should. I wanted to create a twenty-first century version to include engraving for enamelling, my working methods and ideas. Writing this book has enabled me to fulfil my ambition to produce a point of reference for craftsmen, not only established engravers and enamellers, but also people interested in the practical elements of the craft.

This book focuses on the skill of champlevé, covering all aspects including equipment and tools, and describing the making of a piece from idea to completion. It is illustrated with images of finished pieces and of the step-by-step processes, which I hope will both inform and inspire future generations of enamellers.

My father and teacher, Charles 'Fred' Barnes.

Silver engraved and enamelled beaker entitled 'We can not direct the wind but we can adjust our sails'. Designed, engraved and enamelled by Phil Barnes.
90mm high, 65mm wide.

CHAPTER 1

Identifying Enamel and Champlevé

A good place to start would be to make perfectly clear what is meant by 'enamel'. The word 'enamel' derives from the Old French *esmail* and Old High German *smelzen* (to smelt). As a term, enamel has been loosely used to cover some materials that are actually paints, lacquers or resins, but this is not the 'enamel' with which the chapters in this book are associated. The enamels covered here are vitreous enamels, vitreous meaning 'to fire': they can be described as a comparatively soft glass, not unlike the type used in the making of stained glass windows, and have a melting temperature of between 750 and 800°C (1,414 and 1,472°F). It is a compound of flint, sand, potash, lead, borax and silica. These materials when melted together give an end result of a clear frit or glass known as 'flux'.

During manufacture various colouring metal oxides will be added to this frit, the recipes varying according to the different colours and shades required. For example, a blue will have a cobalt oxide included, or a green may have a variant of chrome oxide, with Purple of Cassius, a form of gold oxide, added to make reds. When re-heated, fused and cooled, and poured out over steel plates, the end result of this process is slabs of coloured glass. These slabs, broken up, ground down in a pestle and mortar into fine particles, applied on to a metal surface and then placed in a kiln and fired, will fuse and adhere to that metal base.

This is a brief description of the type of enamelling that will be covered in this book. Enamels come in three different types: transparent, opaque and translucent (sometimes known as 'opal enamel'). A way of describing this further is to imagine three wine glasses, two filled with water and the other with milk. Light passes easily through the first glass filled with water and the water is as clear as glass: that is our *transparent* enamel. The glass with milk has no light penetrating through at all: this is the *opaque*. Add a little of the milk into the second glass of water and the clear water turns into a semi-clear milky liquid: light does pass through, but not to the same degree as the glass containing only water – this is the translucent or opal.

Molten enamel being poured during production at Milton Bridge Ceramic Colours Ltd, Stoke on Trent.

'Alfred Had Me Made': the inscription along the edge of this ninth-century piece, the Alfred Jewell AD871–899. Image © Ashmolean Museum, University of Oxford. AN1836P.135.371

THE HISTORY OF ENAMELLING

The art of enamelling has a long recorded history: the oldest known pieces of enamel work are Mycenaean. In 1952 six gold enamelled finger rings were discovered in a tomb in Cyprus at Kouklia, and a royal gold sceptre decorated with enamel was discovered in a tomb in Kourion. These pieces are the earliest examples of enamel in existence; it is uncertain whether the craftsmen who carried out the work were Mycenaean, Cypriot or Egyptian, but it does indicate that enamelling was first practised in this area as early as the thirteenth century BC.

The history of enamelling can be traced even further back, with instances of enamel work occurring from across the Roman empire; ornamental enamel work can be seen from Anglo Saxon Britain, with the Sutton Hoo treasure dating from the seventh century; and also in Britain, the ninth-century Alfred Jewell was discovered in 1693 at Newton Park, Somerset – it can be seen today at the Ashmolean Museum in Oxford. The piece bears an inscription which in translation reads 'Alfred had me made': the central enamelled section in cloisonné depicts a figure holding garlands of flowers in each hand, thought to be that of King Alfred the Great who reigned from 871–899. The Victoria and Albert Museum in London have many pieces of champlevé enamels which date from the eleventh century and are of religious origin displayed in their medieval gallery.

Champlevé appears to have been the preferred technique of that period, and the piece shown here, the Becket Casket, made in Limoges, France between 1180 and 1190, illustrates this. The casket is made of

The Becket Casket, Limoges, France, AD1180–1190. An example of early religious champlevé. © Victoria and Albert Museum, London

copper, engraved and enamelled, gilt finished and fitted over a wooden case. It is thought that the casket was made to hold the relics of Thomas Beckett, taken to Peterborough Abbey by Abbot Benedict in 1177.

The art of enamelling has gone in and out of fashion during its history; it saw a revival with masters such as Peter Carl Fabergé, famous for his jewel-like gold and enamelled Easter eggs, heavily decorated with engine turning and enamel work, and produced under the patronage of the Russian royal family. The 1900s saw the rise of the Art Nouveau movement, with beautiful enamelled jewellery from Parisian designers of that time such as René Lalique and Lucien Falize. Enamel work today is still popular, freelance practitioners and

contemporary designer craftsmen producing fine examples of this ancient craft. The processes used by today's enamellers are virtually the same as their predecessors, though of course there have been improvements, today's enamels being more stable and reliable.

Developments on the mechanical side, especially with the kiln, have been significant: kilns once heated by charcoal developed into the muffle kiln heated by coke, which gave way to gas and electric kilns, while today's kilns benefit from greater heat control, better insulation and a cleaner environment in which to work. But as regards technique, the basic process of preparing the enamel, the laying and firing and final finishing have remained virtually unaltered.

The Technique of Champlevé

This book concentrates on the technique of champlevé. Techniques in enamelling all bear French names, the reason for which I have never discovered, despite research – it is possibly just one of fashion, and because France was the centre for enamel work for many years. The term 'champlevé' translates as 'raised field', and involves the creation of a cell which is then filled with enamel. There is no specific way in which the cell has to be fashioned – in fact there are many ways they can be created: by using a steel die and stamping out the cell, by acid etching, by machine routing out, and by using today's technology of 3D printing and laser cutting.

My approach to champlevé is to create cells by hand engraving: I recess these to a certain depth with the use of brightly cut engraved lines – this creates textures that bring design and line to the cell, and refracts the light, bringing the colours of the enamel to life.

Gold and enamelled ring with green jade centre stone, engraved and enamelled for Elizabeth Gage Ltd.

OTHER ENAMEL TECHNIQUES

While this book covers just one technique, that of champlevé, there are several other styles of enamel work. A quick résumé of a few of those techniques is given below.

Bassetaille: A low relief design is engraved and carved below the enamel surface. When enamelled over, these differences of depth give variations of colour due to the variations in the thickness of the enamel, giving a monotone effect with darker shades showing in the deeper areas, and lighter shades of the colour where the enamel is closer to the surface.

Cloisonné: Fine examples of cloisonné come from China and Japan, where this technique has a long history. Designs are created by bending and forming fine wires to create the cells, which are then applied to an enamelled base and fired; when the enamel becomes molten the wires sink into the surface, and on cooling are held firm. Enamels, which are generally opaque, can then be applied and graded to finalize the design, taking the enamel and the metal wires level to one surface.

Enamel painting, sometimes called 'Limoges style': In this technique, metallic oxides similar to those used in the making process of enamel are mixed with oil and painted on to a prepared enamelled surface. The colours will mix as any other painting medium, and can be thinned down to a wash to give subtle effects. An enamelled painting is built up in layers, and fired in between each layer; therefore many fires are required to create a finished piece. This technique was often used in miniature portraiture.

Guilloche: In this technique a metal base is engine turned, a process in which a regular repeated pattern with a very bright cut is created. There are two types of engine-turning machine: a rose, or round machine, and a straight machine. The cutter of the machine is controlled by thumb pressure. While a pointer follows a steel pattern bar, moving the piece to echo that pat-

18ct yellow gold and diamond clock. Guilloche dial enamelled for Roger Doyle Ltd.

tern, the engine turner applies the cutting tool, making one cut at a time. With a click of a ratchet dial the piece moves along one cut width, and the process is repeated to form a continuous, regular bright surface. Generally a plain colour is laid over an engine-turned surface, and many examples of commercial work of this type can be found in antique shops. The biggest exponent of this type of work, with many fine examples, is Carl Fabergé, the great Russian master goldsmith.

Plique à jour: This translates roughly as 'light of day' or 'letting in daylight'. This technique is created by the enamel being suspended within an open framework, giving the effect of a miniature stained-glass window, with the light passing freely through it. Fine examples exist from the turn of the twentieth century, with such masters as René Lalique and Lucien Falize.

CHAPTER 2

The Beginning of a Piece

As a designer maker, one of the most frequently asked questions is 'Where do you get your ideas from?' This is a simple enough question, but is maybe not as straightforward to answer, because the reason is, you just don't know. A walk along the beach with the dog, going through the woods or a beautiful sunset, or a postcard found in a second-hand shop, a visit to a museum, a detail on the side of a building – any of these places or things could spark an idea, which will develop and grow into the beginnings of a piece.

Another designer maker once said: 'You don't wake up in the morning and say "I think I'll be creative today!" – you are constantly creative, and an idea can come at any time, often at three o'clock in the morning when you are trying to sleep!' Those early thoughts start to develop and grow, and if you sit down with a pencil and paper and rough out designs, the idea begins to take shape. In this book I use a piece I have made called 'the Dunwich Bowl' to illustrate the path of a piece from beginning to end.

STARTING THE DESIGN PROCESS

The Dunwich Bowl came to life from what was seen one day while walking the dog along the quiet beaches of the Suffolk coast. The sky was a cloudless brilliant blue, the headland lined by wild plants that flourish in that salty habitat. Different coloured pebbles were catching the sun as the waves moved back and forth. What you take in with your eyes begins to stimulate ideas, which progress into the next day, and so you go back on that beach again, this time with a camera, taking shots of things that had somehow clicked with you the day before.

Later, in the workshop, with the camera images printed out, you start the design process, juggling around ideas and images as the first layouts of the piece begin to take shape. These develop as work continues and you make drawing after drawing, altering and refining each one until the final design is there, and you are ready to move on to the next stage.

The Dunwich Bowl: silver, engraved and enamelled centrepiece illustrating the flora and fauna of the Suffolk coastline by Phil Barnes. 180mm wide, 110mm tall.
PRIVATE COLLECTION

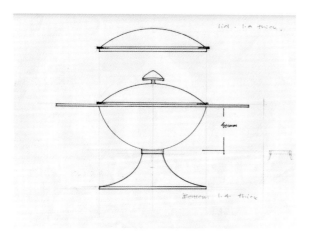

Working technical drawing for the Dunwich Bowl.

First stage in production: all the spun sections for the Dunwich Bowl together for the first time.

CHOICE OF MATERIALS

The practical side of how to make the piece is next: the choice of materials, what thickness of metal will be required, aspects of construction – even the kiln and the size of the firing chamber will have some influence on construction and will have a bearing on the eventual size of the piece. For an engraved and enamelled piece the construction is important: get these early stages wrong, and the results will reflect that, so you must think through every part of the process and try to eliminate any foreseeable problems before you start.

For example, the Dunwich Bowl is made using .925 standard silver, because it is more resilient than fine silver at .999; although the latter is cleaner and has fewer problems with fire stain – we will touch on this later in the book – it does have the drawback of being very soft. For a practical piece such as a beaker, which may take a lot of handling, this softness can be a problem, particularly during the enamelling process, when the risk of the silver moving may result in the enamel bending and even cracking. Thus the thickness of the silver you choose to work with will depend on certain aspects of your design – size, for instance, in that the bigger the piece, the thicker the silver needs to be. And

if the piece is to have engraved cells, recessed all over for enamelling, you will need to make sure the silver is thick enough to allow for this.

On average the gauge to choose would be 1.2–1.4mm thick. A recess for enamelling would be engraved down to a depth of 0.3mm, so the actual base to be enamelled over would be 0.9–1.1mm. Start with too thin a material and problems could arise as work progresses: it is always better to allow for this at the start, and not find out later that you have made the wrong choice.

METHOD OF CONSTRUCTION

The next thing to consider is the method of construction. An enamelled piece, even the simplest of pieces, will go through a firing process at least four times, while a more complicated piece will perhaps have as many as twelve or fifteen firings. On average an enamel colour will fire at approximately 750°C (1,414°F), and with each firing the piece goes into a kiln set at 1,000°C (1,832°F): the higher kiln temperature is there to ensure a rapid fire to achieve better results, so the choice of which solder to use in construction is important.

Silver discs all ready to go to the spinners.

Stefan Coe, master spinner at work.

Wooden patterns are made in the shapes over which the silver sections will be formed.

There are generally five melting points of silver solder to choose from: extra easy, easy, medium, hard and enamelling. The solder to use is the hard, as anything below this will only melt and re-run in the kiln during firing. The other choice would be enamelling solder, although this has a working temperature very close to the melting point of silver, so close in fact that when working with it there is the danger of melting the silver itself. Because of this, the soldering process is often cut short before a good, well fused joint is achieved. However, it is better to ensure a good solid joint with hard solder and be confident of the strength of that joint, than risk damage to your piece with enamelling solder.

Other ways of joining sections together could be with screws, chenier tubing or wire pegs. An enamelled piece should also factor in the possibility of future damage, in the event of the client having an accident with the piece and needing to have it repaired, or worse, re-enamelled. If the design is made up of separate components then each section can be removed, repaired and then re-assembled without causing too much disruption. Sometimes the shape and construction of a piece comes first, with surface decoration and its design being the second stage of the process; in this case concerns may arise that the cost of construction will affect the economics of the project, and it is worth

The three sections of the Dunwich Bowl back from Stefan Coe.

considering different forms of manufacture to help with this problem.

Spinning a shape can be a good option. Spinning is where the metal is pushed over a wooden former with the use of a spinning lathe, which creates the shape quite quickly. Silver spinner Stefan Coe, who spun the Dunwich Bowl, is a master in his own right, and can push and roll silver into any shape or form needed. You can see this from the image of the basic sections of the Dunwich Bowl. The bowl is made up of three pieces: the base trumpet shape, the bowl itself with the outer rim, and lastly the lid. These pieces have been spun from different sizes of circle, and have no soldered pieces on any of the main sections – even base foot wires and bezels for fitting the lid were spun from the one circle of silver. Then all that was needed to finish construction was to make a large base screw for the bowl section, a cover plate for the trumpet section, and the amber top knop.

This helped to minimize the time spent on construction, leaving more time to spend on the engraved and enamelled design of the surface. Something that becomes apparent when designing for three-dimensional pieces is that the true feel of the design does not come alive until you see it on the actual piece; two-dimensional drawings transferred to the three-dimensional shape never look right, and the only answer is to take your idea and draw directly on to the shaped surface. Allowances should be made for this in your initial design work, and you should be prepared to have to adapt and bend the design to better fit the shape.

EXPANSION AND TENSION IN METALS

Every metal has a different co-efficiency of expansion, and it is even more important to understand this as an enameller than it is as a metalsmith. A metalsmith can reshape a piece if there is movement during heating, but once enamelled this movement is much more difficult to correct, and may even be impossible. It means taking into consideration that when a piece of metal is annealed, soldered or warmed in any way the structure of the metal will expand, then contract on cooling. As a general rule the finer the grade of the material, the

more movement the metal will have, and that is found across the board, with silver, gold, even copper.

The higher the percentage of alloy that is introduced into the mix, the more resilient the metal will be to movement. For example if we take .925 standard silver, this is .925 parts of fine silver to .75 of fine copper, both of which must be considered as quite soft materials. However, the result of mixing them together is in fact the opposite, and the silver becomes far tougher than logical thought would have you believe. This change will be found in nearly all metals, especially relating to the metals that we enamellers use.

The Problems of Expansion

So why should this be a concern? As an example, take the case of working over a flat sheet in standard .925 silver. When the enamel is first applied, fine individual grains of enamel are laid on to the surface, and as the piece begins to heat up, the metal will begin to expand. At this point the enamel grains can adjust to any movement as they are only at the first stage of fusion, but take that fire to its conclusion and the result will be that the enamel, although still very hot, goes from a molten to a solid state quite quickly. Whilst the silver is still cooling it is retracting to its original state, causing the enamel to exert a 'pull' on the surface, which in turn causes the silver plate to dome and rise.

With the next fire and the application of a second coat of enamel, once again the silver heats up. The existing enamel, now in a solid state, expands and contracts, as does the metal, but not at the same rate as the silver, resulting in a greater degree of 'pull', so the plate 'domes up' even more.

When planning the construction of a piece this problem of the difference in the rate of expansion and its effects needs to be given great thought. To be able to counteract this effect one of two things can be done: either choose a thicker material with enough resistance to prevent this movement; or the piece can be 'backed' or counter enamelled.

Counter enamelling is the application of enamel to the back of the piece to equal the pull from the front, with the aim of neutralizing this action and keeping the piece flat. Counter enamelling works well, making the form stronger and more resilient, and cutting down on surface movement – however, in a lot of cases it is not practical, nor aesthetically pleasing. It may be acceptable to counter enamel on a plaque or a box top where the back will not be seen, but when working on a piece of jewellery it doesn't look good, so increasing the thickness of the material is the only solution.

The Problems of Tension

The movement between metal and enamel will create tension, which can build up as each layer of enamel is applied and fired. This can result in the enamel cracking, or worse, chipping off altogether as the metal tries to pull itself back to its original shape. While enamel does have some flexibility, it is not flexible enough to withstand this tension, resulting in this cracking and chipping. Using thicker material will of course help, but this tension can remain in the piece for some time, even weeks after the piece has been finished.

This problem is not necessarily due to a bad choice of metal thickness: it can go right back to the design stage, and the decisions made then regarding how to construct the piece. As well as the gauge of the material, uneven thickness can also mean that the metal will not expand at the same rate throughout the piece, the thicker material heating and cooling more slowly.

Another problem that can arise is where areas are unable to move because they are held firm, thus not allowing the natural expansion and contraction process to happen. The following description of a piece that was worked on illustrates this.

The piece was an 18ct gold diamond-set butterfly brooch; the two wings were attached to the main body, each wing being 40mm in length and 15mm wide at the point where they were attached. But when enamelling was under way a problem arose, in that every time the enamel got beyond two coats, each wing would crack and the enamel would chip off about 20mm up from the body; despite trying different approaches, this problem persisted. The solution was to remove each wing and enamel it separately, and to reattach and fit it after enamelling using small screws. This worked perfectly, and there were no problems at all during the enamelling process.

What was learnt from this was that because the lower section of the enamelled wings were held tight and couldn't move easily, the expansion and therefore tension was deferred higher up the wing to the point where there was least resistance, causing the cracking and chipping. It is possible to identify when a crack is due to tension because it will follow the form of the piece – thus a straight edge will show a straight crack, while a curved edge will show a curved crack. If a crack is going outwards from an edge it is more than likely that the damage has been caused by dropping the piece, or by some outward pressure, maybe whilst polishing or during the setting process.

Making sure the enamels are applied thinly will help, as a metal will accept a gradual increase in tension far more readily than if the enamel is applied in a thick coat. When firing flat plates, place them down on to a thin piece of firebrick or honeycombed solder block to fire, and leave them on the brick to cool before removing them: this will help to cut down on movement and keep the build-up of tension to a minimum.

Some shapes are in themselves stronger and will accept more enamel without causing a problem: for instance, enamelling round a band or a domed shape where the pull is evenly balanced, will be far more forgiving than a flat plate.

It is important to make sure the piece is annealed before enamelling, because any material that has been worked, chased or spun will be tight, and the structure needs to be relaxed.

Understanding and thinking about these problems at an early stage, and simple preparation in considering all these small things, will help towards making a piece successfully.

CHAPTER 3

The Engraving Workshop and Equipment

Champlevé can be a very time-consuming technique when hand engraving is involved, with the engraving part of the process, the major element of the work, often taking some 90 per cent of the time involved. It is therefore important to create a place which is both comfortable and practical to work in. A workbench at the right height and a good adjustable supportive chair are both very important if you are to spend many hours engraving. Maintaining a good working position will be of great benefit, not just in the short term but also for future years.

Lighting is another area that it is essential to get right. Working with some daylight is preferable, but will still need the addition of a good artificial light source, because it is vital that you can see clearly the piece you are working on – if shadows are created during engraving they can be deceptive when cutting a line or trimming up a detailed area.

The use of a suitable type of magnification is also something to consider seriously. Even though your vision may be good, you will find that magnification will allow you to work in finer detail. The jeweller's loop or Optivisors (magnifying headbands) come in varying strengths of lens, so the choice is there to suit your needs, and their strength can always be increased

as needed. The double lens of the Optivisor system over the single lens of a jeweller's loop may be preferable to ease the strain of working for long periods using just one eye.

Some engravers and stone setters are moving over to working with high-powered microscope lenses, which can be the static type or headband mounted. However, the cost of these will be high, so consider before purchasing such a piece of equipment, and ask yourself if your work would benefit from this.

THE RIGHT WORKING POSITION

You will know when you are in a comfortable space – or to be more precise, you will know when you are not. Neck ache and back aches may appear after a short spell of working, you may have problems seeing and focusing on the piece: these symptoms will make themselves clear if you are not comfortable.

A useful piece of equipment is a rotating engraver's ball vice. The heaviness of the lower section gives a solid weight and cuts down on movement, taking a lot

The engraver's bench.

The author at work.

The use of sandbags can help raise the piece to a suitable working height.

of pressure off the holding hand when engraving. The upper section has adjustable jaws, which will accommodate most things, and it can rotate and move – it can be adjusted from being completely locked down, to a free revolving action. It also has the benefit of raising your work closer to your eye line, helping to reduce some of the stress in the neck muscles.

The alternative to using a block such as this would be to use sandbags. One or two sandbags laid on top of each other would give you some height, though not the benefit of the rotation the ball vice can give – and no help at all to your holding hand, which will have to absorb most of the pressure during cutting. As opposed to inscription work, engraving for enamelling involves heavier cutting and more push: the amount of metal removed at every cut with a flat scorper is far greater than a square graver cutting a single line, and will therefore take considerably more effort.

The various bench tools of an engraver; you can see that different sized handles are used to adjust each tool's length.

OTHER TOOLS AND EQUIPMENT

The following tools and equipment will be found on the engraver's bench:

- For the preparation of gravers you will need a grinding wheel, a medium-sized bench vice and a hammer
- For marking out and laying down designs: small and medium dividers, a small right-angle square, a steel scriber, a flexi-steel edge, pencils, plasticene and Sellotape, and also wooden-ended and steel burnishers

- For the preparation of the metal surface: small and medium files, an emery stick and emery paper, oil stone or diamond sharpening stones, a power hone for setting up tools and to maintain a good cutting edge, also fine polishing papers for polishing the backs of the gravers when needed, small texturing punches, a repousse hammer
- For holding the work: anti-slip mesh, wooden blocks of varying shapes and sizes, setter's cement or Thermoloc

All these items will appear later in other sections of this book, with their uses explained further.

Half round.

Flat scorper.

Spitstick.

The tools that haven't been mentioned so far are the gravers themselves. These can be broken down into three main categories: half rounds, flat scorpers and spitsticks.

Tool numbers given relate to the size of the tool itself: for example, a size number 4 will be 0.4mm wide, a size 10 will be 1.0mm, and a size 14 will be 1.4mm wide.

Half Rounds

A half round is a round-bottomed tool used for the initial outlining of the design when recessing; it is also used for texturing. The U-shaped cut of a polished half round will give a bright reflective surface for your enamel, and the wider the half round, the more reflective the cut will be. All the main tool types come in various sizes, and increase in size in increments of two. A number 4 or 6 would be a good choice for first outlines, with numbers 12 to18 as texturing tools.

Flat Scorpers

Flat scorpers are the workhorses of the enamel engraver: their only job is to remove metal. They look like small, flat-bottomed chisels, and are used firstly as a cutting tool, and secondly as a scraper for smoothing down the bottom surface of the cells. Again they come in different sizes, and it would be recommended that you have a broad range of these, from a number 2 at the narrowest through numbers 4, 6, 8, 10 and so on, up to a number 18, and then a 24 at its widest.

Spitsticks

A spitstick can also be known as an onglette, and is a tool used mostly by stone setters; however, for champlevé work it is used to trim down the side walls of the cells and to sharpen up angles and corners. When you look at a spitstick front on it looks like the bow of a ship, pointed at the bottom with gently curved sides rising to the top of the tool. To trim back the walls of a cell the side of the spitstick is used, while to put in and sharpen up corners and points, the bottom tip of the spitstick is used.

Sizes once again vary: for enamel work, heavier spitsticks are preferable and reduce the frequency of points breaking off while working. The smaller spitstick will be necessary for smaller, finer detailed work. The two sizes that should cover most tasks are a number 0 (1.65mm) as the smallest, and a number 5 (2.65mm) as the larger. Be careful when ordering spitsticks, and look at the dimensions of the tool over the tool number stated. The numbering of these tools is not the same as flats or half rounds, and different manufacturers can have different numbering systems.

As well as the three shapes above, the following tools would be good additions to your tool range: the knife tool and the square graver.

Knife tool.　　　　　Square graver.

Knife Tool

One medium-size knife tool would be enough in your tool kit; the name is an accurate description of the tool itself, whose two angled sides meet at a sharp bottom face like the cutting edge of a knife. This tool makes a very fine, sharp cut, and can be used for defining small breaks in lines and for putting in fine detail. Although it is not a tool that is used a great deal, it is still worth having.

Square Graver

The square graver and the lozenge graver are the tools of inscription and decorative engravers. They come in different sizes, but unlike the tools above the only cutting point of these is where the front and two faces meet. The choice of size will depend on your type of work or just personal preference – for example, the small size of graver, 1.5mm square, is better for fine work, as any heavy pressure will cause the steel to bend and lose some of its control, while a tool 2.5mm square is more robust and will cope with heavier work. Generally the square graver for the enamel cutter is used for the outline of designs, for making copper plates for repeated

A square graver being used to outline the initial design on the Lion's Head Beaker.

prints, for the bright cutting of surface detail, and for fine lines in texturing under enamel.

When you buy any of the tools above you will have the option to go from the basic steel range of tool up to the HSS, or 'high speed steel' tools. HSS tools are made with harder steel, with the aim of holding the cutting

The Owl Beaker. A silver-lidded beaker, carved and engraved with an enamelled owl feather design by Phil Barnes.

edge longer, so reducing the need to sharpen as often. If you are working on harder materials, such as some white golds, this may be of some benefit, but given that these tools in some instances can be 50 per cent more expensive, if your main work is with silver or softer metals, this could make the extra cost unnecessary.

GRS ENGRAVING SYSTEM

This system will not be found in all engraving workshops, but is becoming more widely used for both engraving and setting. The system works on the pneumatic principle of compressed air pumped into a specialized hand piece, creating a consistent light hammer action into the cutting head and the cutting edge of the graver. The stroke, and therefore the fineness of the cut, can be adjusted according to the type of work in hand.

The necessity to push, as with a traditional graver, is not required, with the tool going forward under power from the system itself; the only concern is therefore guiding the tool's cutting face. Because there is no forward pressure involved, the risk of slipping is greatly reduced. The amount of power and the strength of the cut is controlled by a foot pedal, and the system can be adjusted from 400 to 800 strokes per minute as required. Cutting tools are fitted into separate holders, which are easily interchangeable into and out of the hand piece.

Tungsten carbide tools are available for the system, which can be very useful when working on hard materials, such as steel or white gold, because they will keep their point longer, thus reducing the necessity for repeated sharpening. These tools will need diamond-impregnated sharpening stones to maintain a cutting edge as normal sharpening stones will not be sufficient. This is not a replacement for engraving by hand, especially when it comes to champlevé work, but when working on larger pieces it can help by easing some of the workload, and should be considered as an addition to the workshop's versatility.

Detail of the carved, engraved and enamelled owl feathers.

CHAPTER 4

The Preparation of Tools for Engraving

All new tools will come in a standard size, and it doesn't matter which type of tool it is – half round, flat or spitstick, it will need work to get it to how it is needed before use. If the tool is too long or too short for the hand it will affect the work, and ultimately the results. No two people's hands are exactly the same, and there will be many variations – why would a tool bought off the shelf at a standard length work for different sized hands? Basically it doesn't, and all tools need to be set up for the individual hand size.

Handles come in different shapes and lengths; as a tool wears down, change handles, going up to one of a longer length, so still maintaining the correct size for your hand. During the lifetime of a tool you may change the handle three or four times. New engraving tools will have no lift, by which is meant they cut at a virtually flat angle, so it is better to use flat-bottomed handles so the engraving angle isn't impeded. If flat-bottomed handles are not available to buy, use round handles and saw off what you don't need.

FITTING THE TOOL TO YOUR HAND

Lay your hand flat on the bench with the palm facing up; it must be relaxed, and not forced open. Place the tool and the handle on your hand so that it sits from the soft pad in between your little finger and your ring finger, and crosses at an angle, finishing in the middle of the top pad on your index finger, allowing approximately 20mm for where the tang goes into the handle (the tang is the blued, tapered end on the tool). This will give you a good working length.

Cutting the Tool to Size

Having worked out the right length of tool, next it will have to be cut to size. Any cutting needs to be done from the tang end, which is the blued, tapered end of the tool. Cutting the length to size from this end will maintain as much of the working end of the tool as possible. Mark your length with a marker pen, then using your grinding wheel's edge, cut in, working from both sides, a little at a time; do not grind all the way through – you want the surplus end piece to bend off, not break off. If you grind all the way through in one go, there can be a danger that the cut off section is shot back out at you by the speed of the wheel; therefore grind little by little, testing the end of the tool by pushing it sideways against the bench until it reaches the point when it will

An engraving tool being prepared on a grinding wheel.

The engraving tool should fit from just inside the ring finger to the middle pad of the first finger.

With the tool lying flat on the bench, pinch the tool around 2cm back from the top between the thumb and the first finger.

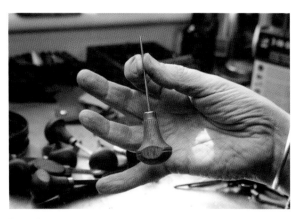

Turn the hand over and let the tool fall back towards the palm.

If the length is correct the tool should fall into place between the two fingers.

That initial pinching action shows how the tool wants to be held when engraving, with the fingers on the side of the tool and not underneath.

Grinding Wheel Health and Safety

While using the grinding wheel, take the normal precautions as when working with any fast-moving machinery: no loose clothing, hair tied back, remove bangles and rings. Because small particles of steel are thrown out from the wheel during grinding, the use of goggles or a visor is recommended. Be aware that the steel will get very hot as it is worked, especially at the tang end, so always keep some cold water close by to cool the tool down as you work. Also make sure that you have a good light source so that what you are working on is clearly visible.

bend easily. Then just keep bending backwards and forwards until it falls off.

The tang end of the tool will have been worked on by the manufacturers and will have a tapered shape. After cutting back the length we will need to re-taper the shape in order for the tool to fit into the handle. Restore the taper with your grinding wheel. It is not important if this end becomes blue – turning blue means that it has become over heated and has softened; however, during this setting-up process it is important that the cutting tip isn't allowed to blue.

Once this task is accomplished – the tool length established and the taper replaced – either photo copy the tool, or draw around it on to a piece of paper and keep this aside for future reference. *But don't forget to allow for the length of the handle!*

Silver engraved and enamelled brooch. Gaudi-inspired design set with an amethyst by Phil Barnes.

Silver engraved and enamelled brooch with Dendrite centre stone by Phil Barnes.

Round silver engraved and enamelled 'Peacock' design, with gold-mounted garnet by Phil Barnes.

Setting up a Square Graver

Setting up a square graver differs slightly from the procedure described above. The cutting action of this type of tool is more static than the flats, half rounds and spitsticks used for recessing, so allow another 20mm or so to the length of the tool when setting up. The square graver requires a lift to be able to cut properly. This lift is created by putting 'backs' on the underside of the tool. A back with a rise of 5 degrees would give enough lift for general engraving work, but this angle can be adjusted to suit.

To create this 'back', place one of the undersides of the graver flat on the sharpening stone, and raise the angle of the tool to around 5 degrees; then with a gently circular motion, wear down until a facet is created. Do the same on the other underside. It is important to make sure that the two facets meet in line with the centre V on the back of the tool. This angle can be adjusted upwards to make the cutting angle steeper, which will be needed for getting into the inside of a bowl or high-sided vessel, for example.

Handle shape will be down to personal choice: some engravers prefer the larger, round ball type, others the half-mushroom shapes that are available – but whatever you choose, it is important to fix the tool into your handle correctly. It isn't a case of banging in the graver like a nail: you need to take it slowly. Place the new graver vertically into a vice with the tang end protruding: if it is a brand new handle, drill a small guide hole for your graver to sit into; if it is an old handle that is being re-used, plug up the existing hole by using matchsticks hammered in until firm, then cut off any surplus.

Push the handle on to the tool to start with, and give it a light tap with the hammer, just enough to hold it in place, making sure it looks straight and level; then give one or two firmer strikes. Do not hit it home fully yet. Then remove the tool from the vice, lay it down on the bench and check it over, looking at all angles: is it level? Is it in straight? If all looks good, then replace the tool in the vice, tighten up and apply firm strokes with the hammer until it is held tightly in the handle.

Next work on the cutting end: the purpose of grinding this end is to remove the bulk of the steel so that when sharpening the tool the sharpening stone does not have so much work to do, making sharpening a quicker process, and less effort. Once again it cannot be emphasized enough *not* to blue this end, as this will soften the steel, and you would then need to go through the process of re-hardening and tempering the tool.

Always use plenty of water when using the grind wheel. One tip is, if you can see water on the end of the engraving tool, then it must still be cool: watch this closely, and keep a water supply very close by – so grind a little and plunge the tool into water, grind a little more and once again plunge into water, and repeat this action until the tool reaches the desired shape.

SHARPENING THE TOOL

Sharpening the tool is the last part of this process. Diamond steel sharpening stones are excellent for this; they can be a little more expensive as compared to a conventional oilstone, but they will outlast these by some time, and will always maintain a good, flat working surface. Keeping the tool sharp is important: trying to make controlled cuts using a blunt tool is impossible. To test if a tool is sharp or not, touch its cutting tip gently on to a finger nail: if the tool is sharp it will catch, just holding into the nail, but if it is blunt it will not, and will just skid over the surface.

With the stone laid on the bench vertically, place your arm alongside, going with the stone: hold your tool at a right angle on to the stone, and lift the back end up at an angle of approximately 45 degrees. Move your arm forwards and back along the stone, using as much of the length of the stone as possible. This arm action should come from the elbow and not the wrist, as every time a turn is made there is a tendency to

Lay the hand parallel to the sharpening stone.

Hold the tool at a right angle to the sharpening stone, and raise to an angle of 45 degrees.

Hold the tool firmly between the thumb and first finger.

'strop': to roll the wrist and so roll the surface of the tool. Imagine the wrist held in a steel band which has no movement, so when a turn is made it helps cut out the chance of rolling the face of the tool.

To see if the tool has sharpened, run a finger lightly along the underside of the tool: if a small burr at the tip has been created then that is sharp, but if no burr is felt, continue.

Lastly, with one quick action, dig the face of the tool into a piece of wood: this will knock off that small burr, because if it remains it will affect the effectiveness of the cutting; this done, the tool is sharp and ready for use. While engraving check every now and then to see if the tool is sharp, don't wait until the tool has worn down or the point has gone.

If you are using a conventional carborundum type of stone to sharpen your tools, you will need to use an oil as a lubricant. However, do not use oil with the diamond steel for sharpening as it clogs the surface. The finer tools will get hot during sharpening on this type of stone, so a small amount of water to help keep the tip cool will help, while on the heavier tools nothing will be required. To help maintain the life of the diamond stone, make sure to scrub off the surface every so often with some soapy water; this will remove any leftover dust and particles of steel that accumulate on the surface.

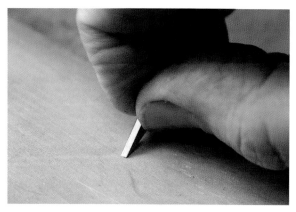

Place the tool down on to the sharpening stone surface, making sure it is sitting flat.

Keeping the wrist as steady as possible, move the tool up and down the length of the stone using long strokes.

To test if the tool has sharpened, run a finger lightly along the underside of the tool: if it is sharp, a small burr should be felt.

If a burr has been created, make a quick stabbing action with the tool into a piece of wood to remove the burr: if it is left on it will affect the cutting action.

Keep a Tool Sharp

It is very important to make sure the tool you are using is sharp, for control and ease of cutting through the metal. With tools like the square graver, knife tool and spitstick, it is easy to see if they are blunt because the point of the tools will have broken off, but with wider and larger tools, such as the half rounds and flat scorpers, this is less obvious as they just wear down with use, so check the tool regularly and make sure it is always sharp when working.

To tell if a tool is sharp or blunt, hold the tool lightly, and let it rest against a finger nail: if sharp it will catch, if blunt it will not.

Silver engraved and enamelled 'Willow Pattern' plate by Phil Barnes. 120mm diameter.
PRIVATE COMMISSION

POLISHING UP A TOOL FOR TEXTURING

Engraving for enamelling is about two things: firstly, creating the recesses in which to place the enamel; and secondly, adding texture to the surface, not just for interest, but also to reflect light back out through the enamel, giving it brightness and life. The tool shape mostly used for this is the half round, as the U shape of the tool will make a reflective cut; however, it will only do this if the surface of the tool has been polished – if left unpolished, the cut will appear dull and lifeless.

To polish, work the back of the tool along a medium grade of emery paper, starting with a 2/0, then up to a 4/0: this will do the bulk of the work, removing scratches and lines created in the steel during the tool's manufacture. For the next stage, use a very fine paper or Micro-Mesh: this is a tough, flexible, rubber-backed polishing cloth, available in four grades, ranging from 3,600 grit up to 12,000; working down these grades, ending with the finest, can achieve a beautifully polished finish.

Having spent the time polishing this tool, keep it just for texturing – don't just throw it back on to the bench with the other tools to get scratched and marked again, but place a cork over its tip and put it aside for the next time it is needed. For everyday general use, make up a second tool that will not require that polished finish.

Occasionally you will need to put a lift on to the tool in order to be able to work a piece properly, in the same way as for the square graver mentioned earlier in this chapter. Generally a flat or half round will cut at a virtually flat angle, but any piece with a concave surface or with a raised rim will make engraving for enamel difficult, and for these, a lift on the back of the tool is required in order to engrave successfully. For tools such as the flat scorper this is easy to achieve, and the sharpening stone can be used to raise the back of the tool to the required angle.

For half rounds it is a lot more work, and you will need to use the grinding wheel to form the tool, and then finish with carborundum stones to produce a curved, scimitar shape. Some engravers will heat and soften the tool and bend it into the shape they want, but this way can be unsatisfactory, the problem being maintaining a balance between the hardness and softness of the steel along the whole length of the tool when it comes to re-hardening.

Sometimes it will be necessary to put a 'lift' on the cutting edge to allow engraving into tight and concave shapes.

WORKING WITH THE PIECE AND HOLDING OPTIONS

The action of cutting for long periods can result in sore joints and neck pain if you can't maintain a good working position. The ideal position when engraving is to have the elbows raised off the bench: like this you can engrave clean curves and lines in one continuous arc. This is easier said than done, however, and the bad habit of resting the elbows on the bench can easily develop, so use sandbags to raise the cutting position and help lift up those elbows, bringing the piece closer to eye level and helping to ease neck and shoulder aches.

As previously mentioned, an engraver's ball vice can be of use here. This is a heavy, universal rotating ball vice, which not only lifts the piece higher off the bench, but also takes some of the pressure of the constant action of cutting from the holding hand. The weight of the ball stops any movement, and being able to lock down or open up the degree of rotation is a great help.

Also give serious consideration to the seat you use: pick one which is height adjustable, and preferably with an adjustable backrest and seat, too, so you can adjust your seating position to the task in hand. How to hold the piece to engrave also needs thinking about. Using just finger pressure to hold a piece of work is not a good idea, as hands and fingers will get tired over time, resulting in slipping; it is better to use a block mounted with setters wax, clamped into an engraver's vice, as this will hold the piece firmly and securely, easing the pressure on your fingers.

An engraver's ball vice has weight and can fully rotate, which can help hold the piece while engraving.

To set a piece into setters wax, warm the piece, not the wax. The warm piece will melt itself down into the cold wax.

Push down lightly and move around until the right place is reached. Be careful not to get the piece too hot.

The piece needs to just bed into the surface, no more; when in position, cool under a running tap.

Setters wax, or jewellers wax as it can be known, is like a sealing wax, which to give toughness has been mixed with plaster of Paris; when this is broken down into small pieces, placed on to a wooden block and melted, it will make a good reusable surface on which to work. Make the blocks deep with the setters wax, so that if, say, you are engraving a brooch with a joint and a clasp, or a pair of cufflinks that are the spring-back type, these fittings can be sunk into the wax out of the way so they do not interfere with the engraving.

To set up, warm the piece to be engraved over a gentle heat, and place it on the wax; the warm piece will melt the wax and settle itself into the surface. When positioned in the right place, put the piece and block under a cold tap and the wax will harden. The hot wax will stick to the metal and give a good bond with which to work. To remove the piece when done, just reverse the process: heat the piece gently over a flame, and lift it off when the wax starts to move.

To remove any unwanted wax from a piece, leave it to soak for a short time in any propriety paintbrush cleaner: white spirit doesn't work well for this, neither does acetone, leaving a greasy surface, but a commercial paintbrush cleaner such as Polycell works well, softening and melting the wax. When finished, wash under a warm tap and brush out with a detergent mix.

Note: Put a warm piece into cold wax, not a cold piece into hot wax, because as soon as a cold piece of metal comes into contact with hot wax it will cool down the surface immediately and a good bond will not be made, with the piece likely to come adrift as it is worked.

When placing the piece on to wax do not let it sink too far down, because if the wax becomes higher than the piece of work it will interfere with the action of dropping down the back of the tool to reach the right cutting angle. Try and make a slightly raised island on the block with the wax, so the tool can drop down easily; any surplus wax that stands proud of the piece can be shaved off with a wide flat scorper.

The Yoxford jewell. Designed, engraved and enamelled by Phil Barnes.

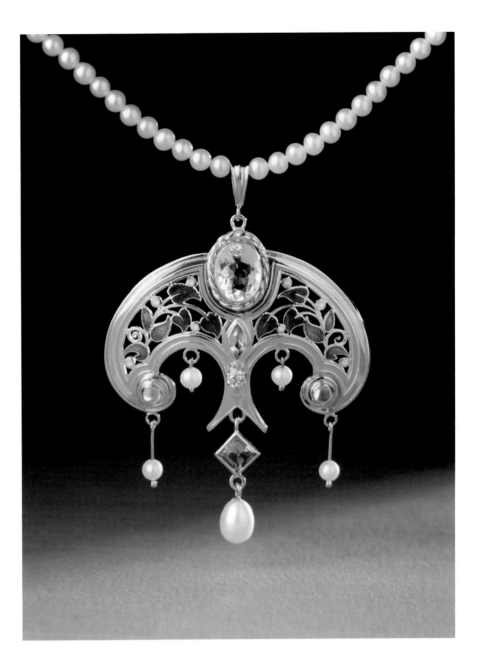

Warning: Hot wax can cause very nasty burns, so it is advised that you wear a glove as protection during this process.

An alternative to setters wax is Thermoloc. This product softens when placed into boiling water or when heated with a hot air gun, going from a hard plastic to a soft plasticene-like substance, which can be modelled and shaped into any form needed to give support. Then when placed into cold water it turns back into the hard surface it started out as; to remove the piece the process is reversed. The benefit this material has is that a direct flame is not involved in the setting up of the piece, so for example in a piece where precious stones are set, there is no possibility of causing damage. Thermoloc doesn't adhere to the surface of the metal as setters wax does, so be careful how the piece is mounted.

CHAPTER 5

Transferring Designs and First Cuts

Earlier chapters have covered the preparation of tools, sharpening them, and all that is required to get started with engraving. We will now look at the cutting and the use of the tools themselves, and at the process of engraving a cell for enamelling and adding a texture. The first task is to mount the piece to be worked on, on to the wax block, as described previously, ensuring it is fixed firmly on to a block that feels comfortable for you to hold. Even if the piece you are to work on is rectangular in design, a block with round or curved edges will be more comfortable to handle than a square block with sharp right-angled corners that will dig into your hands while you work.

With the metal and block ready, the first task is to put down the design on to the surface to be engraved. If the surface isn't too badly marked, use an emery paper or emery stick to go over the surface: this should be enough to achieve what is needed, but any heavier marks may require a light file before starting with emery papers. The surface needs to be even and smooth with no heavy scratches, bumps or dips; a high polish isn't important – a fine papered finish is ideal.

Engraving for enamelling is part of a progression, and many individual cuts will go into creating a cell; that cell will then be enamelled, stoned, lapped and polished before it is completed. A piece of inscription or decorative engraving will require a polished surface to begin with, as in most cases a single cut is the finished article – the piece may have many single cuts to make up the completed design, but apart from a final polish it will have no more done to it.

Marking out the design accurately is essential: if you are vague with what is wanted, the results will be vague, so take the time to ensure that what is put down reflects the final design. This is where it is really helpful to use dividers, square and steel points, and of course the pencil! Set the dividers to the required border width, and run these around the outside edge; then find and mark a centre line of the piece, and put in some light guide marks for help when marking out.

Drawing on the design with a pencil will in a lot of cases be enough, but there will come a time when you need to transfer a design from paper on to the metal. Individual engravers will have different ways of doing this, but the method of using tracing paper, pencil and Sellotape works well and is worth looking at.

Three 18ct yellow gold pins with bronze rabbit details from the fourth century, engraved and enamelled for Elizabeth Gage Ltd.

TRANSFERRING A DESIGN

First copy the design on to tracing paper: this can be ordinary artist's tracing paper, but a plastic tracing film known as architects' drafting film works better, as it is more resilient than tracing paper. It is a plastic film with one dull side, and it will withstand more robust treatment than paper; if kept it can be used again for future projects.

Once you have the design traced, cut off a length of Sellotape that covers the area you want to transfer. Sellotape comes in different widths, so it is a good idea to keep a range in the workshop to fit different sized designs. Place and push down the tape over your traced design, then take up a wooden burnisher – or the end of a small wooden paintbrush will do equally well – and rub it over the surface of the tape, covering all the pencil marks. When done, peel off the tape carefully (this is where the plastic architect's film works better) and you will see that the graphite from the pencil has been taken up by the Sellotape, creating a transparent film of your design ready to put down on to the surface of the piece you are working on.

Carefully put this print to one side, then taking a fine emery paper, rub over the surface of the metal to give it a bright, regular appearance. Next, take up a piece of plasticine, and roll this over the bright surface, leaving it with a dull, whitish look. Pick up the Sellotape print and place it over the area where you want the design to be; using the guidelines put in earlier, place it down into position. Then take up the wooden burnisher, and rub it well over the surface until all areas are covered. Gently peel off the tape, and you will see that the graphite that was held on the tape has been transferred down on to the surface. Make any necessary adjustments with the pencil, then go over your design with a steel point.

This method of using Sellotape has several advantages: the film itself is clear, so it is easy to see exactly where the print is being placed down, and the tape is flexible so will bend over a curve or into a concave shape easily.

The following sequence of pictures shows how to transfer a design.

Items needed for transferring designs.

Architect's film is a form of plastic tracing paper.

Lay the film over the design to be transferred.

Using a soft graphite pencil, trace the design.

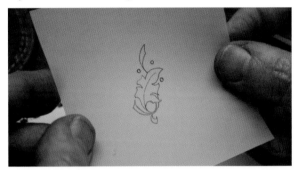

Check over what has been traced; make sure that all the lines that are needed are there.

Take a piece of plasticine and roll it over the metal surface, leaving a whitish film.

Take a piece of Sellotape, enough to cover the design.

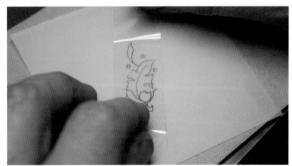

Place the tape down over the traced area.

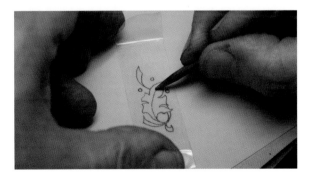

With a wooden point, rub the tape down.

Tip: Making a Tracing

Tracing paper is perfectly adequate for taking a print, but if it is rubbed down too hard it can tear when the Sellotape is removed. Architects' film is more resilient; it is plastic-based and even with vigorous rubbing down will not tear. It can also be used again. Use a relatively soft lead pencil when making the tracing, as the more graphite transferred across will ensure a better print. An HB pencil works well, as it is soft enough but keeps a point, enabling finer lines.

Then peel off the tape from the architect's film.

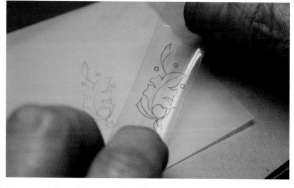

The graphite of the pencil will now have been transferred to the Sellotape, making a print.

Place the print down into position on the metal surface.

Take up the wooden point and rub the print down, then peel off the Sellotape from the surface.

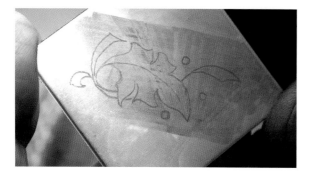

The graphite print will have been transferred on to the metal surface.

With the scriber, go over the pencil lines.

If the design for the piece has a repeated section, first engrave a copper plate with the lines you need using the square graver. When this is done, go over the surface with the steel burnisher to remove any sharp burrs. Then take up a fine black powder – an artist's black powder paint will do the trick, just make sure it is of a fine grain – and rub this into the engraved lines. Once again place Sellotape over the engraved plate, rubbing it down as before; when this is removed you will have a fine black outline of the design. This can then be placed down and repeated as many times as necessary. The copper plate can be kept and used again and again.

TRANSFERRING A REPEATED DESIGN
USING A COPPER ENGRAVED PLATE

Engrave a copper plate with the design to be repeated.

Take up a fine black powder, and rub it into the engraved lines; remove any surplus.

Cut a piece of Sellotape to fit the design.

Lay the tape over the design, and rub a wooden point over the surface.

Peel off the tape from the engraved plate.

The black powder will have been transferred on to the tape, ready to be put down where needed, as described earlier.

CREATING A MIRROR IMAGE PRINT

Another benefit with the Sellotape method is when working on a balanced design, something with a distinct left and right, for example a pair of butterfly wings. On the copper plate mark down a central line, then draw and engrave just one side of the wings. Take a print from that half, and place it down on a flat surface print side up; place another fresh piece of tape over the original print, and rub down well: when peeled apart you will have an exact reverse of the original, which can then be put down in place. When using the print-on-print method, turn back one edge on one of the pieces of Sellotape – if both surfaces get together it can be a tough task to separate them!

With bigger pieces and designs spread over larger areas it is better to work in sections than try and do the whole thing in one go; as long as there are marked guidelines and it is clear where individual sections sit, then all should work well. With a larger piece, which will be handled a lot as it is worked, lightly engrave the lines of the design using the square graver; this avoids the problem of the scribed lines becoming rubbed out and the design losing definition.

The following sequence of pictures shows how to make a reverse print.

Take off a piece of Sellotape and put it to one side.

Take a second piece of tape, and repeating the steps shown previously, create a Sellotape print.

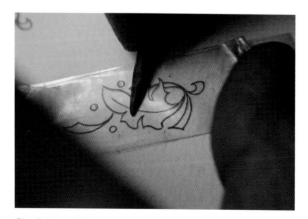
Carefully lay this down on to the piece of tape put aside earlier, and rub over the surface with the wooden point.

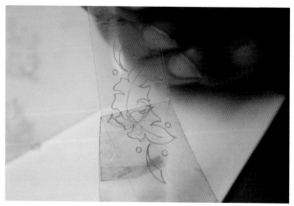
Then peel carefully apart.

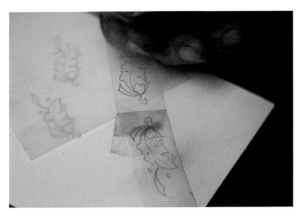

The graphite from the pencil will now be on both pieces of tape.

This gives an exact left and right print of the design.

MAKING THE FIRST CUTS

With the design all marked in, engraving can begin, though before starting check that the tool is sharp, as described in Chapter 4. To start off with, use a half round number four to outline the edges of the design. For the purpose of this part of the chapter the cell described to be recessed is a simple rectangle shape; this will give enough detail of the process that must be followed to take forward for use when engraving future cells.

In the previous chapter that discussed setting up the tools, it was mentioned where the tool must sit in relation to the hand. The cutting action of the tool comes from the back of the hand, from the muscle that is adjacent to the small finger: the push to create the cut will come from there.

It is important to hold the tool correctly. Lay the tool on the bench with the cutting face down, then with the thumb and first finger, pinch the tool about two centimetres back from the top; lift the tool up and turn the hand over, letting the handle drop back towards the palm: if the tool is at the correct length it should fall in between the little and ring fingers, and when the hand is turned back over again, this will have created a tunnel with the fingers. This is what is needed, not the front fingers wrapped completely around the tool grasping it as if it were a screwdriver.

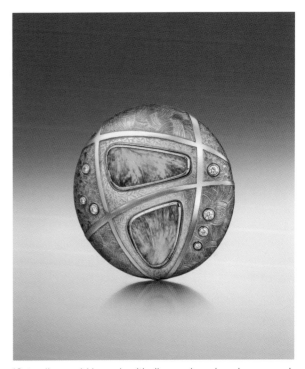

18ct yellow gold brooch with diamonds and opals engraved and enamelled with graded colours for De Vroomen Design Ltd. RICHARD VALENCIA

As a cut is made the thumb will act as a brake, pushing either against the edge of the piece, or downwards on to the surface: should the tool slip, this action should help to keep any damage to a minimum. The first or ring finger is pushing the side of the tool against the inside

Silver engraved and enamelled table salt. The base has a repeated border pattern which is engraved in low relief; also an enamelled bowl and spoon, and a lid in a Paisley design. Designed by Phil Barnes. 110mm wide, 40mm high. PRIVATE COLLECTION

of the thumb, so the action when starting to cut a line is that of the tool running along the thumb. The hardest thing to describe is the amount of pressure required to make the tool go forwards: if the tool is sharp it will not be much, and in time the degree of pressure needed will be easier to recognize – but initially it will be a case of try it and see. If you get it right the tool will move easily, but get the angle wrong and introduce too much pressure, and it will just dig in and grind to a halt.

Place the point of the half round on the *inner* side of the scribed line of the cell to be cut, not on the line or on the outer side of the line, but sitting parallel to it. By working from just inside the design means when the cell is trimmed up and finished it doesn't grow outside the shape required, also by being precise it will cut down the need for so much trimming work with the spitstick when finishing off.

Gently raising the back of the tool, let the point just dig into the surface. As mentioned before, these tools do not cut until they are almost level, so gradually lower the back of the hand until the tool begins to move, at which point do not drop the hand any further, but begin to apply some forward pressure and let the tool move on. While the tool is moving and *under control*, keep going, but if you feel that you are beginning to lose control, stop pushing, raise the back of the hand slightly, and with a quick upward movement lift off the burr that has been created. Place the tool back again in the line where you stopped, and repeat the same action.

It is not a problem if a longer line is made up of many smaller lines – in time you will be able to cut a long line, but the end result will be the same. If the tool keeps slipping forwards as it begins to cut, the likely problem is that the back of the hand is being dropped too far, so the tool starts to lift off like a plane taking off on a runway. It is therefore important to get the feel of when the angle is right, when the movement starts, and when to push.

As a beginner to this type of work the following simple exercise is a good one to work on. With your dividers mark out two sets of lines about two centimetres apart, then with the action described above start cutting from one line, moving across to the other. This will help get the feel of the cut, and is also good practice for stopping and starting.

ENGRAVING THE OUTLINE

Continuing with the engraving of the cell, trace around the whole of the design with the half round, reversing direction and cutting back into the corners, making sure that they, too, are at the same depth. Then repeat the process once again, placing the tool into the cut already made and going over it for a second time; this will ensure a regular solid outline ready for the next stage.

When going over this line a second time the cutting action can be changed slightly: instead of making individual cuts, place the tool in the existing 'tramline' of the first cut; then with the tool at the right cutting angle, move it forwards, and without lifting the tool from the piece, roll it back slightly on itself and then move forwards again. Keep up a 'Two steps forwards, one step back' action as the tool moves around the outline. This solid outline defines the design, ready for the next stage of using flat scorpers to remove metal.

RECESSING

Picking one of the larger flats to start with is not always the best course of action, and a medium-sized tool will cut through the surface with less effort and be quicker – a number ten flat scorper (1.0mm) would be a good starting tool. The trench created by the half round is the starting point, cutting away from this line towards the centre of the cell. By cutting away from the line you help ensure that this outer wall does not get damaged and altered as recessing takes place.

Letting the flat lean against the wall of the half-round cut, lower the back of the hand and add pressure: the tool will start to move, but unlike the action described before, this time keep the back of the hand dropping and let the cut of the tool just fade up – there is no need for the stop and start action as with the outline. Place the back of the flat once again into the trench slightly overlapping the previous cut, and repeat, cutting forwards towards the centre. If the tool is sharp it should not require a great deal of effort. By repeating this action again and again as described it is possible to build up quite a speed and rhythm, and shows how much metal can be removed with little effort.

It is worth pointing out the part the holding hand plays in this action: every cut that is made needs a resistance, and it is the holding hand that bears the brunt of this work. Also, when working on a larger piece it is not just the hand using the tool that will become tired: you must also consider how you work, and with what aids, such as the engraver's ball.

Once the flat has gone all round and cut from every edge, look then at the centre of the cell and go over that as well, so that all surfaces of the cell are to one cut depth all over.

The aim of engraving a recessed cell for enamelling is to create a smooth, level, regular surface; if the cell is uneven, has high and low spots, maybe deeper at one side than the other, all this will show up when it comes to enamelling. The varying depths will appear as light

Close-up shot of a flat scorper at work.

parts in the centre of the cell, which will result in the creation of a concaved recess.

Keep the tools sharp. While a flat scorper's point will not break off, it will wear down, so make sure to keep the tool at its optimum by using the sharpening stone on a regular basis. Next increase the size of the flat up to a twelve (1.2mm) or fourteen (1.4mm); also begin to ease the amount of pressure and the depth of cut, still removing metal but starting to achieve a smoother surface, reducing the heavier cut marks made so far. Follow the same routine as before, with one pass over the surface with the larger flat, concentrating on easing the heaviness of the cut; the cell by now should be getting close to reaching the depth required, which is approximately 0.3mm.

There is no way of measuring the depth of the cell as you work: it is down to the eye, and knowing what is required for enamelling. Some colours, for instance, may require more depth than others – reds, for example, or pinks, where the colour is laid over a coat of flux to achieve the pink colour: these will require an extra layer of enamel, so will need a slightly deeper cell. All these things must be taken into consideration.

At this stage of engraving the cell we can now afford to cut back in towards the outer edge: having recessed deep enough, the edge will now act as a stop without causing any damage. Make each cut of the tool lighter, so it becomes more of a scraping action, and work over the whole surface, changing the direction of the cuts to avoid putting in grooves, working in a criss-cross movement over the surface.

Lastly move up to an even wider flat – a number eighteen (1.8mm), or even a number twenty (2.0mm), allowing for the size of the piece being worked. This tool will only be used in a scraping action, held more to the front of the hand this time, with very little, if no pressure at all. Use a fast backwards and forwards action, lightly touching the surface and removing very little with each cut, but gradually bringing the cell down to achieve a flat, regular surface.

and dark patches in the colour, so it is important to create that regular flat cell.

In order to help this happen, work methodically: as long as the recessing goes down evenly it should end up an even cell. What you do to one side you must do to the other, so try and go down level by level, and do not move on to the next level until every part of the surface has been cut over. Once you have covered the area to be recessed with a first layer of cuts, repeat, ensuring again that every area of surface is cut over. Keep repeating this until the cut surface area reaches the same depth as that of your first outlined half-round trench.

Still with your flat, go round the edge of the design once again, as was done with the half round at the beginning, setting a depth for the next level; again, cut from this towards the middle of the cell. Sticking to a regime of edge, middle, edge, middle will help keep a regular depth, avoiding the tendency to cut away at the easy

First look over the piece on the block, removing any setters wax standing proud of the piece and in the way.

Mark in the edge using dividers – this will be the line you will trim out to.

Take up a number four half round and cut a line tracing the outer edge, starting just inside the marked line.

Starting with a flat scorper, a number ten, cut from the edge towards the middle, overlapping each cut slightly.

Work over the whole surface to one cut depth, then repeat the process once or twice more until the depth of the half-round cut is reached.

Still using the number ten flat, go around the edge of the cell, deepening the edge.

Moving up to a larger sized flat, a number twelve or fourteen, begin removing metal as before, but easing the weight of the cut, leaving fewer marks.

As the final depth of the cell is close (0.3mm), move up to a broad flat, a number twenty, and skim over the surface using the tool more as a scraper.

When the flat surface of the cell is achieved, begin trimming back the edge to the original mark using the spitstick.

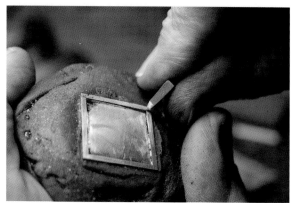

The spitstick is also used to sharpen up corners; any marks made with the spitstick during trimming can be removed with a flat.

Textures under the enamel benefit from being as bright a cut as possible, so it is important that the cutting head of a tool is polished.

The half round is the best tool for texturing, the round cut reflecting more light back. Keep the cuts close together for the best effect.

TRIMMING EDGES AND CORNERS

The last job to finish the cell is to trim the edges and corners; this will be done using the spitstick. If the above work has been carried out correctly there should be very little trimming that will need to be done. Look at each corner: it is usual that each corner will need sharpening up. Taking the cutting point of the spitstick, place the very tip at the point where the two edges meet to make up the corner: do not go outside this, otherwise the whole shape will grow and look wrong. Coming in from the very middle of this angle, make one cut going forward. When you do this you will create a 'V' cut, and the higher you pick up the back of the tool, the more open the 'V' will be; subsequently if you drop the back of the tool, the 'V' will become elongated, so depending on the angle you are cutting, adjust the height accordingly.

To see what you have trimmed can be difficult when you are looking into bright cuts, and to help with this, take a charcoal soldering block, and cut off a piece around 20mm square, which is easy to manage. Rub this into the part to be trimmed: the black of the charcoal will immediately show up exactly where you are, and help you see where your next cut is to be.

Picking up the spitstick, pull the tool backwards into the original cut, making sure to locate it in the original spot, and not to start creating a second corner; this done, turn the piece slightly and cut again, and repeat, fanning out these cuts each way until you have created the square corner that was wanted. Like this, finish all corners, then cutting with the side of the spitstick, trim down the side edges until all corners and sides meet the original scribed lines.

When cutting with the spitstick, do not lean it over on its side too much – the tool itself will already make an angled cut by nature of its shape, and leaning it out more will give a lighter look to the edge when it is enamelled. Keeping the spitstick sharp is important: if the

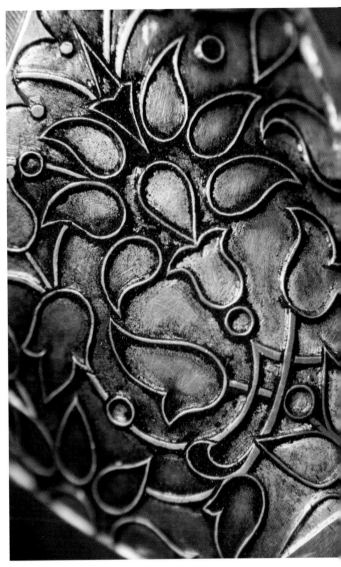

Detail of engraved recess from the floating materials beaker: rubbing charcoal into a piece during trimming makes clear what lines have been created.

point of the tool is blunt, then controlling the direction of each cut can be very difficult.

Lastly, look over the bottom surface of the cell: any marks left in the base surface after trimming can be removed with the flat scorper.

TEXTURING

As mentioned in Chapter 4, putting textures beneath the enamel has two functions: the first is to bring interest into the design; and the second, and more important reason, is to reflect light back from the surface of the metal out through the transparent enamel, bringing light and life to the colour. The more light that can be reflected back out, the better the finished piece will look.

The half round has been mentioned as the tool for texturing, with the round, curved cut of a polished tool reflecting light back easily. However, don't think this is the only shape of tool that can be used: any tool will leave a texture – a flat scorper, a graver, even a burr used in a pendant motor, but unless polished these will not have the same beneficial effect as that of the round cut.

The engraved lines put in when texturing are the finished article, and they will need more precision and control – and the sharpness of the tool is vital. Whenever a tool is sharpened when engraving textures, always finish up by placing the tool down flat on the polishing paper and drawing it back towards you; it doesn't matter how many times this is needed and how well you polished the tool in the first place, always make sure the cutting surface has the best finish it can.

A different look will be gained by using different sizes of tool – thus the finer half round will give a slightly deeper cut than the larger size, and the line will appear a little darker, while the larger tool will reflect more light and appear lighter. Prepare a sample board for future reference, and try different shapes of graver and different types of cut, and try to develop a style of your own.

When making cuts for texturing it is preferable that they sit closely side by side, not overlapping, nor left with gaps in between. Although they may look lovely and bright while all the metal is sparkling and shiny, when enamelled over, these gaps will look twice as wide as they actually are, and this will spoil the effect of the texture. Therefore it is better to keep each cut close and to create a solid area of reflection.

Finish up with a half-round cut following the outside edge; this will give a crisper finish to the piece.

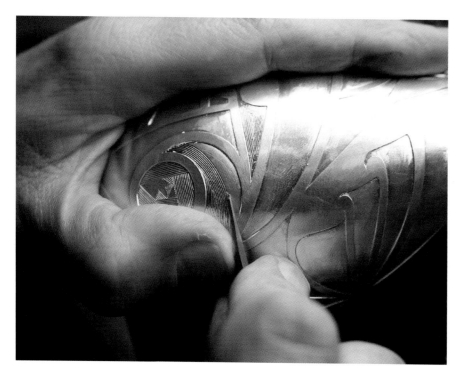

Textures being engraved into the Abstract Design No.1 vase.

Close-up detail of a finished textured section on the Abstract Design Vase: the repeated closeness and change of direction of cut gives a varied reflection as the light hits these different angles.

CHAPTER 6

Metals and Their Preparation

The preparation at the beginning of any project is important; starting off ill prepared will often lead to poor results. To begin with, look at what metal will be used, what gauge it will need to be, how the piece is to be constructed, what solders to use. There are many things that should be looked at even before a hammer is raised or a piercing saw picked up, all of which should be considered at the design stage, as problems can arise that early on in the life of a piece, and can be avoided. A quick conversation between a designer and a maker at an early stage of a project can iron out likely problem areas. It can guide the project in the right direction before the final design is completed, it can make the production easier, and also result in a better looking piece, starting with the metal and what can be enamelled.

My work has always been with precious metals, silver and gold, but there are other metals that will enamel; these will be covered briefly later in this chapter, but this book will concentrate on silver and gold.

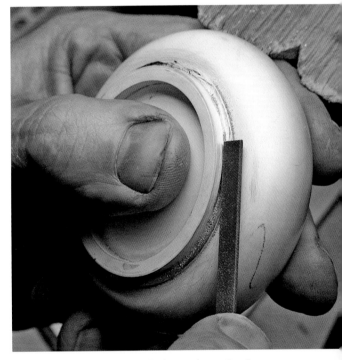

Filing up excess solder from the base wire on the Green Man box.

The Three Lions Head beaker, silver spun form, graded enamels with a repeated design of three lions' heads. The continuous chain motif is carved and oxidized, and the inside of the beaker is polished with a gold-plated finish. Designed, engraved and enamelled by Phil Barnes. 110mm high, 70mm wide. PRIVATE COMMISSION

Silver mainly comes in three grades: standard .925, Britannia .950 and fine .999, and each has its own properties, both good and bad. All these grades will accept enamel, in that during the enamelling process the vitreous enamel will adhere to the surface by means of fusing the glass on to the surface of the silver. To determine which silver is best to use you need to understand the differences in the three grades. The addition of copper into the silver denotes the grade mark: thus .925 standard silver will have seventy-five parts of copper in a thousand parts of silver, Britannia silver will have fifty parts of copper, and fine silver only one part – hardly anything at all, in fact what copper there is comes as part of the natural material. Which metal to use depends on how the different grades may affect the enamel.

First let's look at the good and bad points of these grades .925 standard silver has the highest content of copper and this will affect it in two ways: it will give the metal strength, but will produce fire stain, which if not treated properly will cause problems with your enamels when working with certain colours. (The preparation of the metals prior to enamelling will be covered in more detail later on.) The strength aspect of the addition of copper is its good point, making the silver a tougher material for everyday use and wear. At the other end of the scale, the lack of copper in fine silver makes your enamels appear brighter, and there is no worry of fire stain in the metal as this does not occur when fine silver is annealed or soldered.

Fine silver is often recommended as the only silver to use for enamelling, but this isn't correct; the reason for this assumption is because the way of removing fire stain is not understood. The real drawback with fine silver is its softness. The nature of pure silver is to be very pliable, and if used for a practical object – a piece that is subjected to everyday handling, such as a brooch or a goblet, for example – that piece will be prone to bending and cracking.

Furthermore, when enamel is used over fine silver it will draw up and pull the metal and create ten-sions within it – what may start out as a flat piece will soon take on a gentle curve. But as the piece cools, the metal will want to move back to what it was originally, a flat piece, and this introduces the possibility of cracks appearing as the tension takes hold; and continuing with further coats of enamel could eventually lead to the enamel flying off altogether.

There are two ways around this problem: either introduce counter enamel, where enamel is added to the underside of the piece to equal the pull and to balance out tensions; or increase the gauge of silver to give more substance and strength to the piece, which will not always be practical or aesthetically pleasing.

Obviously .950 Britannia silver falls in between .925 and .999; in this book I will concentrate on .925 and .999 for the next step. Virtually all the silver pieces I work on are in standard .925 silver: this greatly reduces the problem of the enamel cracking and the necessity of having to counter enamel, and as long as the metal is prepared correctly, good results will be achieved.

THE PREPARATION OF SILVER FOR ENAMELLING

As mentioned earlier, problems can occur with certain colours when enamelling with standard silver. Fire stain is a layer of copper oxide that builds up on the surface during the annealing process or during soldering. If left untreated, the enamels will in effect be laid over copper, giving dull, lifeless and dark colours instead of over the clean white surface of silver. Colours such as rich blues are very forgiving, and in most cases will work perfectly over fire stain, but results will be poor with colours in the pale end of the spectrum and with lighter shades. Reds in particular will suffer badly if the metal isn't attended to. For good results on standard .925 silver it is important to remove fire stain before starting to enamel.

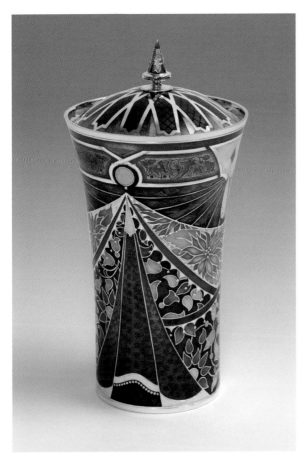

Floating Materials Lidded Beaker. Designed, engraved and enamelled by Phil Barnes. 120mm high, 70mm wide.
PRIVATE COMMISSION

Removing Fire Stain

After soldering or annealing, the silver will have gone from the original white into a dark shade of grey. The most natural thing for a jeweller or silversmith to do next would be to place the silver into pickle. Pickle is a mix of sulphuric acid and water, approximately ten parts water to one part acid (always remember, with sulphuric acid add the acid to the water, not the water to the acid, otherwise there will be a strong reaction, which may be dangerous). After a short while the grey of the silver will go back to the original white.

This will not remove the fire stain, it is more a bleaching process, and the copper oxide is still there as a fine layer over the silver surface. The aim is to remove the oxide, and this is done by using commercial standard nitric acid, which is graded at around 70 per cent, sometimes known as technical grade. Other grades of nitric are available, but for example a grade of 49 per cent will not have the strength to ensure a proper clean.

First, place the piece to be cleaned in a suitable container; plastic sandwich boxes are perfect for this. Pour the nitric acid over the piece until it just covers the surface, and slowly move the box backwards and forwards to create a gentle wave motion. At first there will be no obvious sudden change, and the silver will still look white, but as you continue, the white will be replaced by a grey that gets darker until the surface turns black: this black is the copper oxide, which now we want to remove. Keep up that gentle rolling action, and watch for signs of the black beginning to change: it will turn to grey, and eventually to white. Simply put, the piece will go from white through grey to black, and then back from black to grey to white. If the process is stopped at grey the piece will not be sufficiently cleaned: it must go through to white.

This process can take time, but don't rush it. If the piece has gone through multiple annealing or numerous stages of soldering the oxide will have built up, with the layer of copper oxide being heavier than it would be in a piece that has just been annealed once. In this instance, to help the process, warm the acid slightly. Just adding a small amount of hot water can do this, as a warm acid will work faster, but it is important to keep control. Thus, whilst continuing the rolling motion, tilt the tray slightly and add a small amount of hot water to the opposite end away from the piece. Start again with a wave action, introducing the warmer acid slowly: this should start the process of the grey turning to white, working through until the piece is a clean white all over.

Now wash the piece thoroughly under a running tap, drain it off, and then give it a second quick rinse with clean nitric acid, no added water this time. Wash it again well under running water. If water has been added to the nitric do not put this back in with the clean acid: by adding water you have weakened and contaminated the acid, so it will be no good for any future cleaning of silver. However, this diluted acid is good for any etching work that may be planned, so decant it into a separate jar, mark it clearly and store it for future use. If no water was added, then you can return it to the original jar.

One thing to consider when cleaning with nitric acid to prepare a piece is, the process is in effect giving the whole surface a very light etch, and this means everywhere – front, back, sides, solder joints, fittings, knuckles of hinges, wires and tubes, everything – so take care, because if you do too much, what was once a nice, tight-fitting joint will turn into a loose fit! Taking this into consideration, I suggest that the final fittings or adjustments are left until after enamelling; alternatively

use an acid resist to stop out and mask off these areas so that the acid cannot do too much damage.

If the metal has not been fired, annealed or heated in any way, but is in the same pristine state as when it came direct from the bullion dealer, it should immediately come up that nice, crisp white when placed in your tray and washed over with nitric – it will not go grey or black, so don't continue, stop there.

The 'pickle' mix I mentioned earlier, one part sulphuric to ten parts water, I use cold, not warm. In the enamelling workshop the pickle mix is always used cold because although a warm acid will work faster, it is more aggressive, and this can be too strong for some enamel surfaces. At best it will leave a bloom appearance after pickling, but at worst your enamel will be pitted, as the acid will have attacked the surface.

Two standard silver discs ready to clean: one has fire stain and the other hasn't.

Pour over the nitric acid.

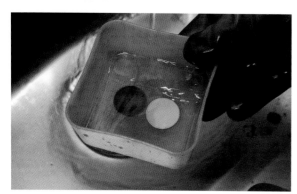

The one with fire stain immediately turns black: this is the oxide showing up. The other has no fire stain and stays white.

Keep up a gentle rolling action, moving the acid over the surface.

The oxide showing black will begin to wash away.

Do not rush this process, just keep up the rolling motion.

Don't stop, even if there is only a small grey area left showing...

...keep on until the whole of the disc appears white.

Wash well with plenty of running water to remove any acid.

The two discs now look identical: neither has fire stain in them, and after brushing over with the brass brush they are ready to enamel.

Pair of 18ct yellow gold, tourmaline and diamond drop earrings. Engraved and enamelled for Henn of London.

CLEANING FINE SILVER AND GOLD

Cleaning fine silver .999 and 18ct gold follows the same process, and is a great deal easier because the problem of fire stain does not arise as there is no copper oxide on the metal – or if there is, it will not be enough to cause a problem. Here the kiln can be used to heat the metal to the point just before it begins to change colour, that soft golden colour. When it reaches that point, drop it immediately into the pickle, while it is still hot. The metal should hit the acid with a *whoosh*, a whip-crack type of sound, not a weak *phut* – if the sound is a soft *phut* it means the metal is not getting hot enough. Repeat this action two to three times and you should be left with a clean bright surface.

This is sometimes referred to as 'depletion gilding', bringing the gold up to the surface, but I feel it is more like pushing the copper content back. Gold, whether it is yellow, white or rose gold, should be prepared in the same way.

Finally, before it is ready to enamel, the surface of the metal will need brightening, and for this use a brass brush – nothing fancy, one that you will find in any jewellery tools suppliers. Using a generous amount of detergent as a lubricant, brush up the surface thoroughly, working into all the corners: this will leave a bright, shiny surface good enough to reflect back light from under the enamels.

Using detergent as a lubricant will prevent any brass being deposited from the brush: not enough detergent, and a faint yellow tint over the surface may appear as brass is picked up from the brush, making all your efforts in cleaning your metals a total waste of time. Washing-up liquid mixed generously with water works very well. Wash the piece well in clean running water, and dry it off with a clean cloth.

18ct white gold ring with Chalcedony Cabochan stone. Engraved and enamelled for Henn of London.

ACIDS

The acids so far used have been nitric acid, for the cleaning of silver, and sulphuric acid made up as a pickle mix, one part acid to ten parts water (remembering to add the acid to the water, and not the other way around). One acid we have not yet mentioned is hydrofluoric 40 per cent, which is used solely for dissolving glass and removing enamel – it does not attack either silver or gold, and the only metal-based substance it touches is lead. There may be occasions when the result of your work is not up to expectations, or when a problem arises, and you need to start a piece again, and it is on these occasions that the hydrofluoric comes into use.

This acid is the most dangerous and aggressive of all the acids used in the workshop, and is capable of producing very serious burns, so protective clothing is a must at all times when handling it.

When you have occasion to use this acid, only bring out what is needed at that time, and store it in an airtight *plastic* container – remember do not use glass, as hydrofluoric acid will dissolve it, and always ensure the container is *well marked*. An antidote gel is available to purchase, and it is highly recommended that this is added to the workshop first aid kit. The acid itself is reusable, so a small amount will generally last a long time: dependant on use, a half litre should be more than sufficient for several years, so take this into consideration when purchasing.

The main thing to remember when working with any acid is to be sensible, take care, understand what you are dealing with, and take all necessary precautions at all times – and then there should be no problems.

The Use and Storage of Acids in an Enameller's Workshop

It is important to be aware of the safety aspects concerning the use of acids: they are harmful, and great care must be taken at all times when handling them, and common sense and concentration when using them is essential. When storing acids, keep them in a

Acid warning sign.

locked cupboard, ideally fire resistant and well marked with chemical hazard warning signs so that it is obvious to anyone what is in there. Any bottle containing acid in that cupboard must also be clearly marked; if any bottle is beginning to lose a label, or a label is becoming faded, make sure it is replaced and shows exactly what that bottle contains.

Always use acids in a well ventilated area. The use of a fume cupboard is ideal, but if one is not available, an area with an extractor and access to fresh air is the next best thing; also, work where there is plenty of running water and clutter-free work surfaces to carry out any process. A protective apron, rubber gloves and goggles must be available, and it is wise to have made up some form of neutralizer in case of any spillage; soda crystals made up to a liquid kept in the form of a spray is useful and should be kept at hand.

If any acid is permanently in use and left out on this working area, the pickle mix for instance, make sure it is clearly marked: a simple hazardous corrosive sticker on the wall alongside as a warning would be a good idea.

For full health and safety measures on the use and storage of acids, go to the HSE website at www.hse.gov.uk; I have also included in Useful Information some companies who produce acids where full SDS safety data sheets relating to the acids mentioned in this book are available; but any search engine will bring up many sites for further reading.

Close-up detail of an engraved and enamelled box top.

OTHER MATERIALS THAT CAN BE ENAMELLED

Silver and gold have been mentioned, but what else will enamel? Copper will also enamel, but not brass or nickel as they have too much zinc content. Silver, mentioned earlier in this chapter, and gold will enamel as long as the gold/alloy ratio is right. In 18ct gold the gold content will outweigh any other alloy used: twenty four parts is pure gold, so 18ct leaves only six parts of an alloy. If that alloy is something that will take enamel, there is no problem at all, but if the alloy used does not, or the ratio changes, then problems can arise.

For example, 9ct gold has nine parts gold to fifteen parts of what? In yellow gold the alloy will be brass, but brass has too much zinc content to enamel successfully, so 9ct yellow gold will not enamel. However, if that 9ct gold is alloyed with copper, as in rose gold,

or with silver, as in white gold, it will enamel, but both these alloys will have a different effect on the outcome of your finished look. 9ct gold alloyed with copper will be red and copper-like, the oxide will scale as copper does, be soft like copper, and give your enamels a dark look, whilst 9ct gold alloyed with silver will appear more straw-like in colour, a pale yellow, and will act like silver when enamelled.

Platinum will enamel, that it is to say the enamel will fire on to its surface and adhere to it. However, because platinum has a completely different expansion rate to any other metal, when it comes to applying and firing more than one coat, the enamel will just crack, making working with this metal extremely difficult. If you look back at platinum jewellery of the past, you will see only small areas of enamel used, mostly opaque, and mostly black or dark opaque blues. Cartier diamond-mounted pieces of the 1920s are a good example.

In the last few years palladium has become a hallmark standard metal. It will enamel, but it will give problems with some colours – reds and yellows, for example, will never look good. One problem that is thankfully resolved with the use of palladium is when working with white gold castings. In the past, silver and zinc were added to make up white gold casting material, and if the balance of the zinc content crept up just a fraction it was enough to make that casting unworkable. Thankfully palladium and silver now replace the zinc content, and this has all but resolved the problem, with very few issues now arising.

WORKING WITH CASTINGS

Castings have improved greatly: better equipment, and a better understanding of materials and new technology have all led to an almost trouble-free process. However, there are some procedures that need to be carried out before beginning to enamel a casting. The biggest problem when working with a casting is porosity, and it is still the main reason for a casting being unsuccessful.

Air trapped within the metal when it is enamelled will result in cracking, chipping and poor surfaces.

The most likely place to find porosity is around the sprue, which is the feeder point for the metal. During the casting process molten metal is fired through this feeder point into the piece to be cast, reaching the furthest points first; it is cooling all the time, and the last place for the metal to complete the cast is around the sprue, so this is where the metal can be less stable, leaving small pockets of air trapped inside. Sometimes this can be very clear to see, with distinct holes and pitting of the surface; at others it may look fine, but only when work is begun on the piece will you discover how bad the casting is.

When I need something cast I leave the adding of the sprue to the caster: he has a far greater knowledge as to how the metal is likely to flow, and where problem areas might be. Whilst not guaranteeing a perfect cast, it will help achieve the best possible result.

If you have any doubts it is always good practice to talk with the caster, and to get his opinion on the pattern and his view on any problems that could arise. Varying thicknesses of metals in the design could be a problem, and size and shape another, so take advice before continuing. Silver castings can be more problematic than gold, resulting in a lower success rate. Fire stain is usually heavier in cast silver, and cleaning can be a problem, with the end results being affected unless a vacuum system has been used, where very little, or no fire stain is produced.

PREPARING A CAST PIECE IN SILVER OR GOLD FOR ENAMELLING

First, warm and quench the piece into a cold sulphuric pickle mix as described earlier; repeat this two or three times. Next, place the piece into a heat-resistant bowl filled with water, enough to cover the surface, and add to this a small amount of soda – these can be crystals, or one of the made-up proprietary brands: both work equally well, just don't add too much as this can leave a film over the metal.

Place the bowl on a hot plate and bring to the boil. Leave for around five minutes, giving the soda and water plenty of time to work into the metal, neutralizing any acid absorbed into the casting. The water may become brown and dirty, and if it does, change the water, add more soda and continue. The water should remain clean and clear. The discoloration of the water is caused by acid and investment plaster within the metal. If there is no discoloration, continue.

Wash the piece thoroughly under running water and brush out well with your brass brush and detergent. Dry off the piece with a cloth and place on a mesh, and warm gently in the kiln. Take it up to a golden look, no more, and not so far that it turns black.

When cool, look over the surface: if porosity is present you will see dark marks or even white powdery deposits. If these are present, brush out again with the brass brush, and repeat the warming process; if necessary repeat again until the surface looks clean.

This process is designed to neutralize any acid and to clean out any impurities from within the casting, and to give as good a surface as you can to enamel over. If you did not follow this process and went straight into enamelling, the fumes and impurities coming out from the casting would badly affect the enamel, leaving a dull surface, and possibly rejecting it completely. If heavy porosity is present, air will be held within the metal, which when enamelled over will trap that air in – then in subsequent fires it will expand and try to make its way out, causing blow holes and pitting, or worse, throwing off the enamel.

When working with silver castings, go through the normal silver cleaning process before proceeding with the above. Be prepared for the occasional bad casting, and order extra pieces to allow for any rejects.

CHAPTER 7

Tools, Equipment and Enamels

THE ENAMELLER'S BENCH

A bench suitable for enamelling should be of a comfortable height with plenty of space to spread out tools and materials; an adjustable seat and good lighting must be the first considerations of any working bench. For enamelling it doesn't need to have a cut-out, just a straight-edged table is fine, but establishing a good, comfortable working height is important.

You will need the following tools and equipment for enamelling:

- Apart from quills, add in a paintbrush, some plasticine for holding the work, some absorbent cotton cloths, a palette knife and tweezers
- China watercolour palette dishes for holding the enamels work well: china has more weight than plastic, and doesn't move as you are trying to work
- You will also need carborundum stones, Diagrit strips, and wet-and-dry emery paper for stoning and finishing
- Always keep a small water bottle on the bench filled with purified water. Every time you finish work with an enamel, maybe to get up to fire or when work is finished, it is good practice to make sure the enamel

is always covered with clean water; also, keep that water refreshed as work continues, to cut out any film or scum developing on the enamel. When returning to enamel, pour off the old water: keep an old jar on the bench for this, and begin a cycle of replacing the water constantly through the working day. If the enamel is left to dry out, or is left sitting in old water, this will affect the quality of the finish – and a simple task such as replacing the water is a good habit to get into
- You will need at least one pestle and mortar for grinding the enamels, and it is wise to have mortars in two sizes to allow for different volumes of enamel to be ground
- Good airtight storage for the enamels in a dry place will be needed: while lump enamels may not be so much of a problem, pre-ground powdered enamels will be, and must be kept dry – any dampness or moisture is to be avoided at all costs
- A label machine in the workshop is a good thing to have for marking enamel jars and pots of enamel, as it is not always obvious what a colour is – a strong golden yellow, for example, may look like a clear flux in some cases, so a clear marking system will help avoid any confusion

The enameller's bench.

Tools and equipment used by the enameller, displayed on an enameller's bench.

- Easy access to good running water is essential for an enameller, and at the sink, make sure you have both brass and black bristle brushes on hand, and a container with water and detergent
- Some strong rubber gloves, protective glasses, long tweezers, and plastic trays and boxes for use with acids
- Up at the kiln, a pair of tongs or a firing fork, whichever is preferred, a pair of large size tweezers, a protective glove against the heat, and if it is a concern, some protective green-tinted, anti-glare goggles
- Some stainless-steel meshes of different sizes, stainless-steel supports, and pieces of thin firebrick or honeycomb soldering block for use when firing flat pieces
- Over time, odds and ends of various pieces of mesh, wire or brick will be collected, but never throw anything away, as you never know when they will come into good use
- A heat-resistant surface will be needed around the kiln area, with a steel block to place your work on, and a brush for keeping the kiln area clean
- Finally, a good light

LOOKING AT ENAMELS

Enamels come in three types: transparent, opaque and opal. Transparent colours are clear, light reflective and bright. Opaques are solid block colours, giving no reflection at all. Opal enamels fall somewhere in between, and have a semi-transparent, pearl-like appearance.

Another area to consider concerns lead or unleaded enamels. With stricter health and safety guidelines, some countries have banned the use of lead in enamels; however, lead in enamel has been used in its production for centuries as it gives the enamel hardness and brightness – think of the qualities of lead crystal glass, which has very similar properties to enamels.

The absence of lead has a detrimental effect on the quality of the finish, and also affects the appearance of some colours. As lead-free enamels generally have a lower firing temperature, multiple firings will not be possible because of the danger of burning out the colour. Acids will affect the surface of these soft colours, also the process of lapping a soft surface becomes a problem.

Silver Tazza dish, designed, engraved and enamelled with graded colours in a random abstract floral design by Phil Barnes. 145mm diameter. PRIVATE COLLECTION

All the enamels I use are lead based; you must decide which kind you choose to work with, but you cannot use leaded and unleaded enamels alongside each other on the same piece.

It is important to understand your enamels and the palette of colours you are going to use in your work. This doesn't just mean what the colour looks like, that is down to personal choice, but there are some practical factors to consider: will the colour stand multiple firings? Will it work alongside other enamels, is the firing temperature of the enamel compatible with the other

colours already used, will it stand going through the pickle? Will it lap, polish and still keep a good surface? All these things need to be looked at. As an established enameller you will have colours you know and trust, and colours that meet all the above criteria. If you are new to enamelling, with little experience of enamels, then there is a need to establish quite soon one or two reliable colours – this will give you a 'benchmark' to test any new enamel against.

Make your initial tests with several colours on one sample plate at a time. Observe closely how they behave in the kiln, which colour fires first, is one a lot harder to fire than the others, and so on. Follow this up with a second coat, and you can begin to judge which enamels are looking good. It may turn out that a blue will be the most reliable, or a clear flux, as both these are generally dependable, but whichever you choose, keep this as your 'benchmark'.

Working samples from Phil Barnes' workshop. The pieces are all in standard silver, stamped from a tool ensuring that samples are all the same size and thickness.

TESTING ENAMELS

Just because a piece is a test piece doesn't mean that any corners are cut in its preparation. Grind, wash, lay and fire as you would if it were a piece of saleable work. Try and make your sample pieces similar in size and thickness of metal: this helps when you come to judging the firing time. Samples carried out half-heartedly on odd shapes and sizes of silver do not help give a true test.

When trying to establish the benefits of a new colour, the first thing to look at is the temperature, using your established colour as a guide. Lay the two samples, one in the new enamel and one in your benchmark enamel, close to each other on the mesh, and fire. Watch constantly as they fire, and gauge the new colour against the established one. If the new colour fires around the same time as your benchmark colour, that is a good sign. If it fires either before or after, then you must assess by how much, and if that enamel is going to work alongside other enamels. If the firing times are compatible, carry on with the test. Put a second layer of enamel over the new colour and fire the sample once again, and when cool add a third coat; this will give you the same amount of enamel as you would lay on to a piece.

Next is to establish if the new colour will stand multiple firings, so repeat the firing three or four more times without adding any more enamel. Take a close look at the results: check the colour hasn't burnt around the edge, that the colour of the enamel is consistent, the surface is good, that there are no bubbles or signs of small holes, something that becomes very important when working on larger pieces, or maybe when working on graded enamels, which by the completion of the piece could have gone through the kiln some ten or more times. The decision then to carry on with the sample can be made against your established enamel.

I will use the terms 'hard firing' and 'soft firing': a 'soft' colour fires more quickly and has a lower firing temperature, and the 'hard' will fire for longer, having a higher firing temperature. So, was the new colour firing more quickly, and if so, by how much? Was it so great

18ct yellow gold brooch, with mandarin garnet and diamond centre. Engraved and enamelled for Henn of London.

that the benchmark enamel was only just beginning to fire? Or was it within a manageable range? Or was it taking longer to fire, so would be considered a 'hard' colour? There will be a range of firing that is acceptable – working from your benchmark firing temperature, a colour can be slightly higher or slightly lower and still work alongside your existing enamels; it is when the range becomes extreme that the problems arise.

If all still looks good, stone down the surface, brush it out, and give the piece its last fire. When cool, place the sample into the pickle and leave until the metal turns white. Then remove it from the pickle and wash well. If the enamel is good, you should see very little difference in the surface, but if you see pitting and a matting of the surface these signs are not good and will raise the question as to whether it is usable. After lapping it should show a smooth, drag-free surface if it is to be added to your palette.

All this work may seem a little excessive, but it is well worth doing, because once you have established that the enamel is good, you won't need to test again until you change batches.

You don't have to keep to using just one manufacturer's enamels: I use enamels from various suppliers, but all the enamels must have the capability of working together. Batches of enamel will vary in production, with no two batches being exactly the same: some may change slightly, while others can show dramatic differences, and you can only guarantee what an enamel colour is like from that batch of production; it is therefore good practice to test any new batch before use.

To try and ensure continuity and quality in the enamels, when a good colour is found, buy enough to last for a reasonable period, allowing for the rate of use. This may mean that only a small amount will be needed, maybe 100 or 200g, while in a busy workshop the amount may

Keep pestle and mortars of different sizes, and choose one appropriate to the amount of enamel to be ground.

be as much as 1 or 2kg – but at least this way you know that if you have a good colour it can be used reliably for some time to come.

When I need to restock a colour, I ask the supplier for a small sample first: test it as described above, and if all is well, then reorder, ensuring it is from the same batch as the sample tested. Enamels are an integral part of this type of work, and knowledge of them and understanding their capabilities is important to create consistently good quality work.

GRINDING AND PREPARING ENAMELS

Every part of the process of enamelling needs to be carried out correctly: if you get one small step wrong it can be the difference between success and failure. Grinding and the preparation of enamels is one of the most important parts of the process, and needs to be done with care. Where possible, try and buy your enamels in lump form – though a lot of manufacturers are now supplying their enamels only in powder form, in response to demand, so lump enamel is becoming less available and harder to find.

Why Lump and not Powder?

The aim for an ideal piece of enamel work is to have a perfect, clean, bubble-free surface. Enamel in its make-up includes metallic oxides, and these can be a reason for the breakdown of that surface if ignored. Once ground or in a powdered form the atmosphere and the water in which the enamel has been prepared can start affecting that oxide. The colour itself will not change at all, but bubbles and pits may appear in your finished surface if that reaction has begun. It is never clear how long a powder enamel has been made, or how long it has been sitting on the stockroom shelf before it has been purchased. Has it been stored in a dry, warm atmosphere, or maybe in damp conditions? Another consideration is how long it has been in the workshop – all these are details that are in most part unknown.

Enamel in lump, on the other hand, will remain in its original state for many years to come, and it is not unusual to find lump enamels in old established workshops that are many years old and still perfectly usable.

The breakdown of a colour is also a concern after the enamel has been prepared. This can depend on the water supply available in the workshop, the length of time the colour is kept for, and also how it is kept – and this can change from one enamel to another, as some enamels can be affected just hours after preparation, while others show no effect days after being ground.

Silver triangular 'Peacock' dish. Designed, engraved and enamelled by Phil Barnes. 180mm diameter.
PRIVATE COLLECTION

Compare this to what happens in other areas where metals are exposed to the atmosphere and, for instance, rust might occur, or the oxidization of silver from the atmosphere alone.

Unless this aspect of enamels is thought about, the problem of bad surfaces and bubbles in the work will always be there. If powdered enamel is the only form you can obtain, at least look at your own storage methods, use air-tight containers, and keep them in a warm and dry environment.

Why Grind Already Ground Enamels?

Grinding down the enamel creates finer grains, which will make laying easier and allow for thinner coats, which will cut down on weight. This alone will make enamelling over shaped articles easier, it will make the grading of colours more effective, and will remove the need for introducing gum into the enamel to help adhesion when working. Enamel falls off pieces before they are fired because of the weight of the grain, the weight caused by the thickness of the coat, and the weight that is in each grain, and grinding the enamel finer will help all this. By adding even a few drops of gum into the colour you are in effect adding a foreign body, something we will touch on when the section about washing the enamel is reached.

To demonstrate this further, take three varying sizes of bead – small, medium and large – and three identical shallow plastic containers. Cover the bottom of these containers with each of the bead sizes, and the first thing that is apparent is the difference in gap size between each bead size, the gaps being larger and more open between the largest beads, but getting smaller and tighter together as the size of bead goes down. Next

The Aldeburgh lidded beaker. The design depicts aspects of the seaside town of Aldeburgh in Suffolk. Designed, engraved and enamelled by Phil Barnes. 130mm high, 78mm at the widest point.
PRIVATE COMMISSION

look from the side, and you will see the difference in the thickness between the layers of bead, where once again the thinnest layer consists of the smallest beads. Lastly, weigh each container: between all three there will be a difference in weight between all three, the lightest being the one with the smallest beads.

Maybe this test is stating the obvious, but if these beads represent the grains of your enamel, ground to different levels, then it should be clear what it is better to do.

THE PROCESS OF GRINDING

All enamels need to be ground, opaques, transparents and opals, it doesn't matter even if it is pre-ground already, it will require more. To grind enamels the best thing to use is a pestle and mortar, nothing special, something that can be purchased in any kitchen shop is fine. The use of an agate pestle is unnecessary, the cost of such and the sizes available are too restrictive, while the porcelain sets are easily available and inexpensive. Pestle and mortars come in different sizes and are available in size one, two and three; it is wise to hold a variety of sizes in the workshop using a size which suits the volume of enamel to be ground. When using a new set for the first time grind for a while with just water in or if you have some old enamel not wanted use that, this will work off any loose or powdery debris left on the surface during production. The first thing to do when grinding a colour is to make sure the pestle and mortar is clean, even if it looks clean do not rely on just looks, make sure, wash under a running tap around the bowl inside and out and every part of the pestle.

Lump enamels may be daunting to start with, and your first reaction may be that it will take a great deal more work, so why bother with lump? However, this is not the case, as long as you tackle the task correctly. Take the lump, and if it has come from the supplier in very large pieces, place it in a clean plastic bag and hit it with a hammer over a steel plate to create small pieces. Then take up some of these small pieces in the hand, and drop one or two into the mortar filled with a little water, and with a sharp, striking action hit the lumps with the pestle repeatedly until those pieces are reduced to the size of coarse grain. Then add a couple more pieces and bang those down to the same level, and repeat, adding the lumps slowly, small amounts at a time.

If the whole batch of lump enamel is put in at one go it becomes very hard to hit individual pieces, with lumps flying off in all directions; tackling it little by little makes the task easier and quicker.

Once all the grains are roughly at the same point, add a little more water and with the pestle in the centre of the bowl, push down firmly with a quick stirring action, exerting pressure in short bursts until a regular sound and feel is achieved. This will only take a very short time – if you have it right, then it will take no more than a couple of minutes to go from lump to grain, something of the size a pre-ground enamel would be. Gently run water from the tap around the edge of the pestle to clear up any larger pieces that may be clinging to the sides of the bowl, leave for a second or two, then pour this off and refill with enough water to cover the enamel, and continue grinding.

How Long to Grind?

The question always arises 'How long should you grind for?' and the simple answer is 'Until it's ready' – it's a 'How long is a piece of string?' question, and will depend on what you are enamelling and the process

you are going to go through. If you were enamelling a single colour, flat plate that is, say, 100sq mm in size, the enamel wouldn't need to be ground as finely as colours you were intending to grade with, or enamels that were to be laid over a shaped or curved surface, possibly with the enamel being suspended upside down, as on a tube or a bangle, for instance.

With experience and with trial and error you will get to know when the enamels that you are intending to use are at the right grain – and you will soon realize when they are *not*. Often you will find that enamels need grinding a lot more than you first thought, but a general rule of thumb is that a colour will take around fifteen to twenty minutes to prepare.

What to Look For

When grinding there are three signs to look for: firstly the sound – as the enamels become finer the sound will drop, becoming quieter, sounding less coarse. Second is feel: slow down the speed of grinding, and, holding the pestle lightly between thumb and forefinger, feel the grain between the pestle and mortar as you turn – the vibrations will transfer themselves up into your hand, giving an indication as to what the grain size is. Lastly is touch: take up some enamel, pinching it between two fingers and gently rubbing them together. Once you pass the first smoothness, the feel of the true grain can be established.

Some enamel will be physically harder than others to grind – for instance, all blues are hard, while opaque enamels are soft – but this doesn't always follow a pattern: it is something to discover as enamels are worked with, but these hard colours will require more time to prepare.

18ct gold and diamond picture frame, with applied diamond-set shells. Engraved and enamelled for Roger Doyle Ltd. 140mm high, 120mm wide.

WASHING THE GRAIN

When the desired grain is reached, the enamel should be put through a process of washing to remove that fine silt created during grinding; if left in, it will have a detrimental effect on your finish, affecting its clarity and the quality of the surface.

Firstly fill the mortar with water, covering the enamel. A good habit at this point is to add one or two drops of clean nitric acid into the colour; it is not an obvious benefit that will be noticed, but it can help. In an enamel you can sometimes get tiny build-ups of oxides that have not properly dispersed during manufacture – these are not necessarily visible with the naked eye, but they can leave dark dots in the enamels. There will also be minute particles of the pestle and mortar that will make their way into the enamels during grinding, and a few drops of nitric can help dissolve these.

One school of thought is that the acid can affect the hardness/softness of the colour, but generally I have not found this to be a concern. It is not essential to add the nitric but it can help, and having a small dropper bottle filled with clean nitric near the grinding area is not a great inconvenience. One word of warning, however: there will be the occasional colour that *can* be affected by the addition of the acid – some opaque reds and some dark greens, for instance, can have an immediate reaction, where the enamel starts to turn black and a pungent smell of sulphur is given off when the acid is added. If this does happen, pour off the water and acid and refill with clean water, which should stop any permanent harm being done to the colour.

Leave the acid/water mix in with the enamel for no more than a minute, then gently pour it off, refill the mortar with water, and leave once again, watching as you go. Repeat this process, noting as the washes progress that the water begins to clear and settle more quickly after every wash. Like the piece of string question, enamel is washed when it's washed, and there is no magic number of washes, but the more finely the enamel has been ground, the more washes it will need.

To establish if the enamel is washed enough, when the water used to fill the mortar settles down almost immediately, and the grain and colour of the enamel looks regular, then it's about there. As one last check on the final rinse, as you gently pour off the water, give the mortar a slight swirl: should you see a 'ghost', a slightly milky wisp appearing in the colour, then give the enamel one or two more washes, finishing up with the very last wash in purified water.

When washing very light colours, fluxes or whites for example, always give a couple of extra washes to make sure it is ready, as these light colours can be difficult to see and it is far better to be safe than sorry.

When the washing process is finished, transfer the enamel into a suitable receptacle ready for use.

The Quality of Water

It will depend very much where the workshop is based as to the quality of the water on hand; for example, where I have my workshop the water is very hard, and the house has a water softener with salts to prevent the build-up of lime scale. Making sure the enamel has its last couple of washes in purified or deionized water will help to cut down any reaction of the oxides within the enamel when exposed to the atmosphere, or when ground. The use of purified water will help to slow this deterioration, giving the colour a longer working life, and will also help to give a better look and finish to the enamels.

When grinding enamels it is good practice to stand, not sit.

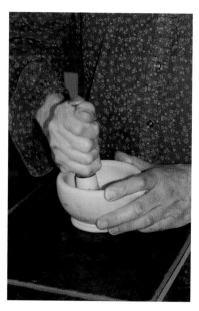

Standing keeps the arm parallel, so most of the pressure needed comes from the weight of the arm.

When grinding lump enamel, break down one piece at a time, adding in as you go.

With quick turns of the pestle, apply pressure into the centre of the mortar.

This will quickly bring down the grains to a workable size.

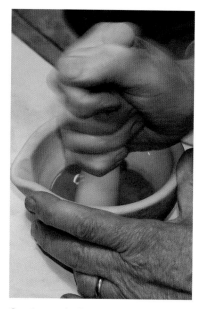

Continue grinding with a steady, regular speed.

Test the enamel as you go: as it gets finer the sound will change; also pinch a small amount and rub it between finger and thumb to feel the size of the grain.

When the desired grain is reached, fill the bowl with water, and allow it to settle.

Settling time will be longer to start with, and shorter as the washing process progresses; pour off the water slowly.

Repeat this process of filling with water and pouring off to wash away the fine silt created during grinding.

The aim is to have a clean-looking, even-coloured grain of enamel. There should be no 'ghosting' in the colour.

There is no set number of times to wash the enamel, and one more extra wash will never be a bad thing.

Outlining the design of the Lion Head beaker with a square graver.

CHAPTER 8

Working with Enamels

For the application of enamel the requirements are very simple: a quill and a cotton cloth. The mode of applying the enamel will come down to personal choice and the way you were taught, and who taught you. As already mentioned, my enamelling background comes from my father and a quill was the tool of choice, as that was used in the workshops where he was trained. You can often tell where an enameller was taught by the type of tool he uses and the way he lays the enamel.

QUILLS AND HOW TO PREPARE ONE

There are many benefits of using a quill as a tool for applying enamels – it is a natural material, firm but still flexible. Try pushing a quill against your fingernail: it has some bend and give, yet when tapped against your nail it seems rigid. Using a steel tool to apply the enamel doesn't give you this flexibility, and there is also the possibility of a steel tool scratching the surface of the metal as the enamel is laid, something a quill won't do.

Phil Barnes at work enamelling the inside of the Dunwich Bowl.

A quill can be cut to a desired shape easily, and it is easy to clean when going from one colour to another – a flick with a finger at the end of the quill removes any remaining enamel, unlike using a paintbrush to lay enamel, when it is difficult to ensure that the fine grains of enamel have all been removed from the brush hairs before moving on to the next colour without the danger of contamination. Best of all, in most cases they can be picked up free of charge! The type of feather doesn't matter, it could be swan, seagull, turkey or goose, as long as it is of a good size, somewhere around 30cm in length, 5 to 6mm in diameter, and has a firm, split-free central core.

First check the feather over to see if it is suitable for use. Roll it between two fingers and at the same time squeeze the main core: if a cracking sound is heard it is split and therefore no good; if there is no sound it is good to use. With stout scissors or snips, cut off the top four inches of the feather and peel off the two sides from the central stem (this part of the feather is called the vane, to give it its proper name), leaving just the main hollow shaft, which is known as the calamus, or quill. Most feathers will have a natural curve to them: holding the curve upwards and the quill end pointing away from you, come down from the end about twenty-five millimetres, and with a sharp blade make one swift cut at a 45-degree angle.

With a pair of snips, take off the feather's last 50–60mm.

Peel away all the remaining feather from the central core.

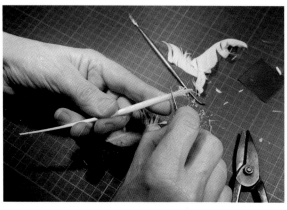

Taking a knife, scrape over all the quill's surface to remove the fine membrane which is there.

Place the knife blade at about 25mm from the top, and at an angle of 45 degrees.

Make one swift cut downwards away from you.

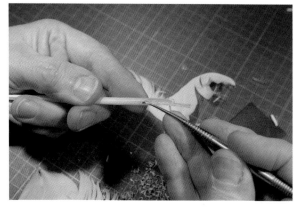

Using a curved-ended tool, put this down into the central core of the quill, twist, and pull out the calamus from within.

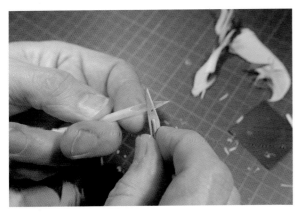

Begin to shape the quill into the thickness required – this can be as broad or as thin as is needed.

Lay the quill end down on the bench, then take the blade and make one cut, removing the very end part of the quill.

This will remove any small splits still present at the point.

Using the back of the knife blade as a scraper, give the quill its final shape.

Take a fine emery paper and go over all the surfaces of the quill and rub them down.

Lastly, wash the newly cut quill well under a hot tap to remove any remaining dirt before using.

Three 18ct yellow gold lion's head pins with Roman bronze heads. Depicting the lion of wisdom, of justice and of nobility. Engraved and enamelled for Elizabeth Gage Ltd.

The last thing to do is to trim the quill down to the desired shape, paring off thin slices at a time from each side of the quill with the sharp blade until the right shape is reached. Finish off by rubbing over all surfaces with very fine sandpaper, and then wash under hot water.

A quill can be formed into a sharp point for working on detailed sections, or given a broad, round end for applying larger amounts of enamel. It is a waste to keep cutting the same quill: a better way is to keep a range of quills cut to cover all aspects of your work, then not only will you have the correct size quill ready to use, but this will also help extend the working life of each quill.

LAYING THE ENAMEL

With quills cut, enamels ready and metal cleaned, the process of applying the enamels is ready to start. If the piece is heavily shaped or hollow, like a bead for instance, it is good practice to warm it well before you start laying the enamel to let any moisture or possible acid fumes remaining evaporate off, so any chance of fuming or bubbling out will not affect the enamelling process. However, if the piece to be enamelled is a flat, open shape this won't apply.

Be aware that the surface of the enamel whilst in its unfired, or stoned and unfired condition is susceptible to picking up the slightest impurity. For example, a finger touching the enamel while laying, or fumes escaping from a hollow object, even being heavy handed with a cloth when drying a stoned piece before the last fire, any of these can result is a dirty white crumbly mark being left on the surface when the piece is fired. The enamelling process cannot proceed unless these marks are attended to and the bad enamel removed, so it is important to bear this in mind while working.

Select a quill to suit the piece – don't use a thin quill to try and lay a large open surface, and equally, don't try and do detailed work with a quill shaped with a broad head.

Inside the calamus there is a tail-like membrane that needs to be removed, and a tool with a hooked end simply made from a piece of wire will do the job perfectly: push the tool down the central core as far as it will go, then twist and pull, and the tail should come out in one piece.

Next, using the blade of the knife as a scraper, go over the whole body of the quill removing any odd bits of feather left behind, and also the fine membrane which is found over the surface.

18ct yellow gold diamond brooch. Engraved and enamelled with graded colours for De Vroomen Design Ltd. LEO DE VROOMEN

Along with the quill you will need a piece of good absorbent cotton around 20sq cm: this is to be used as a method of controlling the ratio of water to enamel as you work. This cotton square doesn't have to be anything special – as long as it absorbs water easily and quickly, it will do the job; it's surprising how many 20cm squares can be produced from an old bedsheet! It is advisable not to use kitchen towel or blotting paper as these two materials have small fibres that can come off into the work, something cotton doesn't do; also cotton can be washed and reused many times over.

Open the top lid of the china palette and place it down on the bench; take the lower section with the enamel in, and with a quick action pour off most of the surplus water, then rest it up against the palette lid, tilted forwards. This tilted angle will show a water line in the enamel, which while working gives the option of taking the enamel grains from above the line, where the enamel is slightly drier, or below the line where the

ratio of water to enamel is greater. The amount of water can be adjusted accordingly as the enamel is worked, just by where the quill picks up the grains of enamel. The biggest part of the enamelling process is to ensure as even a coat as possible as it is applied: it is not good practice to lay the enamel thickly and then try to correct it; it is better to lay thin, even coats.

How Thin is a Thin Coat of Enamel?

The average depth for a cell in a piece of champlevé work is 0.3mm: this will allow for three to four coats of enamel to be applied, so it is here that the finer ground enamel comes in. Coarser, heaver grains will take up more space and will not lie as close together, making the application of thin layers almost impossible; where more detailed work is involved, finer ground enamels are essential.

Enamelling a section of the Dunwich Bowl; a piece could have as many as five or six thin layers applied to create the desired look.

Using the quill open side upwards, take up some of the enamel from just above the water line, then bring the quill closer to the metal surface and gently turn it towards the surface: the enamel will begin to move from the quill on to your metal. Move that enamel around using the point of the quill, spreading the grains as you go, making sure there are no areas of metal showing through.

Repeat picking up the enamel and placing it down, making smooth any unevenness of enamel laid as you go – a gentle tap at the edge of the piece will help slightly to take down any unevenness, but this must not be relied upon to obtain a smooth layer: it is better to achieve this by controlled laying of the enamel.

A good tip for laying is to imagine a piece of tracing paper laid over a piece of metal: it will have some transparency and will have an even look, and you should think of this as how the enamel should appear. If you doubled the thickness of the tracing paper it would appear solid, losing that semi-transparency, and similarly, if the enamel starts to look as solid as this, it will indicate that the coats of enamel being laid are too thick.

Silver 'Graffiti' pendant. Designed, made, engraved and enamelled with graded colours by Phil Barnes.

Continue laying, constantly checking on the amount of water within the enamel as it is worked: if it is too dry, it will become stodgy and will not lay down easily or be easy to move, making it difficult to lay smoothly. If there is an excess of water it will be moving too much, being all water and very few grains of enamel, and once again it will be hard to lay an even coat. In this case we introduce the cotton cloth: just touching the very edge of the enamel lightly with the cotton will draw the excess water by capillary action towards the cloth, bringing it back to an ideal ratio of water to enamel. In the case of it being too dry, start to pick up water from lower down in the dish with the quill, then lightly touch the enamel and the reverse action will happen: the enamel will absorb more of the water and balance out that ratio.

The judgement of balance between water and enamel is the skill to learn here: water is needed to help lay the enamel, but it needs to be maintained at just the right balance to ensure consistency and

good results. If what is being laid is unsatisfactory it is better to stop, rinse it off and begin again, and not to continue to firing.

A problem that may arise is grease on the surface of the metal, which will make the laying of enamel very difficult; grease could have been left from the cleaning process, or could have contaminated the piece if it has been left out uncovered for a period in the atmosphere. This will be evident by the water balling up when attempting to apply the enamel. If this happens, stop, and using the cotton cloth, absorb a little saliva from the mouth, then wipe over the surface to be enamelled. Saliva acts as a natural degreaser, and as long as all surface areas are treated, should solve the problem.

If it persists while you are laying the enamel, breathe out with a heavy breath over the piece, and the moisture from your breath will have exactly the same cleaning effect and will allow the laying of the enamel to progress more easily.

18ct white gold 'bird' pendant with tourmaline centre stone. Engraved and enamelled with graded colours for Henn of London.

Enamel can easily be affected by touching the unfired surface, even with hands that are spotlessly clean, as the natural oils in the skin will cause a reaction. Holding a piece can then become a problem, and how to hold the piece should be looked at even before the enamelling process is started. A pad of plasticine works well for this, because it can be moulded to fit the desired shape, from a flat plate to a curved bangle: as long as there is surplus around the piece to hold, the fingers will touch this, and not the surface where there is enamel.

For bands and ring shanks a screw type of opening and closing ring stick is ideal, while for beads or chain links a piece of stainless steel wire bent into the desired shape will give support, not just whilst it is being enamelled but also when firing.

Once the coat of enamel is down, make sure all surplus water is removed, once again by touching the very edge with the cotton cloth before transferring the piece on to the steel mesh support ready for firing. Firing the enamel is covered in more detail in Chapter 9, but the main point is to watch, and to know what is happening in the kiln: it only takes the odd glance through a slightly opened door to ensure where you are in the process.

Once fired, you can move on to the next coat – there is nothing to be done to the surface other than a wipe over with the cotton cloth, checking first that all looks well and there are no bad areas before continuing. Having got the first coat down successfully, the laying of the second and subsequent coats will not be so difficult, because when laying on to the fired surface it is easier to move the enamel grains around and manipulate them.

Keep to the same principle as before, ensuring a smooth and even a coat, still keeping the coats thin, pushing the enamel into corners and edges so that there is a regular thickness all over. Dry off the excess water, once again using the cloth, and fire for the second time. The level of firing should increase as the enamelling process progresses: quicker and lighter on the first coat, extending the time for the second and subsequent firings, with the last and final fire being the longest. Once again there is nothing to be done to the surface apart from checking over the results of the second coat and wiping over the surface with the cotton cloth.

Continue by slowly applying the third layer; the enamel will be nearly up to the level of the cell, and there is no need to apply any more enamel than is necessary. Use the same procedures as before, dry off the surplus water, and fire.

Enamelling with Pinks

It will sometimes be necessary to put a first coat of flux beneath a colour, pinks especially: if a transparent pink is applied directly on to the metal the results will show as orange. The flux is there to put a barrier between the pink and the metal surface. It is essential that your base layer of flux is thin, and must cover the entire surface where the pink will be. Do not let the flux ride up the side of the cell too much, if it does when it comes to stoning up and finishing the piece you may see that orange tint appearing around the outer edge, so be careful with that first base coat.

Small silver beaker with flowing peacock feathers. Designed, engraved and enamelled by Phil Barnes. 75mm high, 50mm at the widest point.
PRIVATE COMMISSION

Stoning Down and Finishing

With three coats of enamel now laid and fired, the last stages of stoning down and finishing begin. Stoning down is the wearing down of the enamel until it becomes level with the metal edges of the cell. For this process I would initially choose a carborundum stone. Carborundum is a trademark name for a synthetic silicon carbide that has been produced since 1893; it is a man-made, very hard material with particles of silicon carbide being bonded together. These can be purchased in many shapes – square, triangular, even round – and come in varying coarseness of cut.

Using the stone as if it were a file, work the stone over the surface using plenty of water as you go; keep up a constant movement to avoid putting grooves into the enamel surface, and check the surface regularly – what you are looking for is a consistent matting of the enamel where the enamel has been taken down level with the cell wall. When this matting is achieved you can be confident that a flat, level surface has been created; however, if there are areas that remain shiny, it is better to stop any further stoning, and refill those areas with a touch of enamel to bring them up to the level surface.

Whether the cell is full or not, before applying any enamel or continuing to give the piece its last fire it is necessary to brush it well under a running tap with the black bristle brush. This will make sure that all particles of ground enamel and particles of the metal edge are washed well away, leaving the surface clean and ready for the next step. Remember, as stated earlier, do not put your fingers directly on to this surface, just carefully dab it dry with the cotton cloth. If enamel needs to be applied, apply it to those areas and fire, then repeat the stoning until all surfaces are uniform.

Finish up by going over the surface with a fine wet-and-dry paper, around a 240 grade: this will help take out any of the heavy stone marks in both the enamel and the metal surface. Brush well again, and then prepare for the last fire. This last fire, as mentioned, is the longest the piece will receive, as not only does the enamel have to re-glaze, but any lines left in the surface after the stoning process have to fuse and smooth out, leaving a regular, even look.

When cool, place in a mixture of sulphuric acid and water, known as a pickle: this will clean up the metal and bring silver back to white and gold back to its natural yellow colour; always use this pickle cold. Jewellers, goldsmiths and silversmiths use this pickle mix for the same process, but will use it warm to speed up its action; however, because some enamels can be affected by the acid, using it cold will be a lot less aggressive and gentler on the enamel.

When pickled, wash the piece well to remove any of the acid residue before the last stage of lapping and polishing, described in Chapter 10.

ENAMELLING OVER A SHAPE OR CURVE

The main challenge of enamelling over a curved or shaped piece is the ability to control the water-to-enamel ratio – this is far more important than when enamelling over a flat surface as described above. This control will be the difference between failure and success. The weight of the water will want to roll towards the edge of the piece, taking the enamel with it, and so it is imperative to master this control.

Grain weight is another big consideration here. Producing a finely ground enamel has been explained above, where the grains will sit closer together and allow for thinner coats to be laid. With a curved shape the finer grains will also have less weight, so reducing the tendency of the enamel to move with the effect of gravity, pulling your enamel downwards towards the low sections or edges of the piece.

It could be considered that the addition of a gum or clear fire would help bind these grains together and cut down on movement, but think twice before adding either of these to your colour as you may be jeopardizing all the work that has been put in with the washing process. One area that has been made clear is the importance of preparing the enamels well, of grinding and washing them well, and also keeping them under purified water to help prevent any breakdown in their make-up. The addition of a gum into the enamel contradicts this, and should be considered as the addition of a foreign body into the well prepared enamel.

With practice, the control of the enamel will become easier; no enamelling is easy, but as long as the process is not rushed and is approached carefully, results will improve and eventually be mastered. As an enameller starting out working on a first piece over a curve, it would be advisable to ease in gently and start with a metal plate that is just slightly domed, or maybe a ring with an enamelled band, before tackling a larger surface such as a bangle or the inside of a bowl. Irrespective of size the principle is the same, and an easier project will give you confidence before you tackle more difficult and steeper shapes at a later date.

Example of enamelling over a tight curve. The base of the 'Green Man' box has been
enamelled with a rich blue-green to highlight the leaf design engraved beneath the surface.
Designed, engraved and enamelled by Phil Barnes. 80mm diameter. PRIVATE COLLECTION

Laying enamel over the curved base, gradually working around step by step, maintaining an even coat.

It is important to use a cotton cloth to absorb surplus water as the enamel is laid to keep the enamel at the right consistency to be able to work it.

An old carborundum stone that has become curved through years of use is ideal when working on pieces such as this.

Finish up using a fine Diagrit strip, which can bend to the form and help keep the curve of the shape.

WORKING OVER A DOME

When working on a curved shape, notice there is always a flat place, the very top of a ball or a band ring, at that 'North Pole' point – looking side on as if it were a clock dial, the point at twelve o'clock is flat, and if you turn the ring slightly there will still always be a small flat area sitting at this top point. Therefore the important thing to remember is to move the piece as you work to find that small flat area to work on.

Starting with the domed plate, wipe over the surface to make sure it is grease free and ready for enamelling. Then take a pad of plasticine and mould it into the shape of the piece, making sure there is excess material around the shape so it is easy to hold with the fingers without touching the enamel. Place the piece on the plasticine and press down lightly, just enough for it to hold – if you press down too much it will be difficult to remove when enamelled: you want the piece just to sit on the surface and not to sink in. So take care, because plasticine, like fingers, can leave marks if it comes into contact with the enamel.

In the centre at the very top of the curve, lay a small circle of enamel with the quill, about 1cm across: you will see that the enamel stays put and does not appear to want to move. Dry off the water with the cotton cloth, and tilting the plate slightly, begin to lay another small circle alongside, leaving a small gap. When this is done, connect the two together lightly with the quill, working quickly and as smoothly as possible. The first circle will begin to absorb water from the second circle, so with the cotton cloth touch the very edge of the enamel and draw off most of the water, keeping the enamel damp enough to work with, but not so wet that it wants to move.

Keep up this pattern – leave a small gap, lay a new section, connect and draw off the water – all the time moving and tilting the plate so you are always working on that small 'flat' area. As the process progresses the enamelled area will become heavier and will naturally want to begin to roll or move, and it is the enameller's job to control that with the help of the quill and the cotton cloth to maintain the right consistency.

Continue laying the enamel, moving around the piece, working from the middle towards the outside, leaving the very edge as the last section to enamel. When you are done, dry well, and using the corner of a palette knife, ease up the edge of the plate from the plasticine; carefully slide the knife under the plate, lifting it up, then transfer the piece to the firing mesh.

WORKING ON A BAND RING

Plasticine will not work successfully as a method of holding a ring, but an expandable ring stick with a central screw core would. The ring will fit over the top chuck like part of the stick, which can then be tightened – though don't tighten it too much, remember, because as with the plasticine, you have to remove the ring when it's enamelled.

Starting at that 'flat' section again, lay the first small bar of enamel, and then dry with the cotton cloth; like the domed shape, it shouldn't move. Then leave a gap, lay the next small bar and then connect the two, and dry once again, continuing around the ring, moving, laying and drying.

On a sharp curve do not neglect to check what is happening on the areas already enamelled: it is easy to

Tip: Be Prepared

Before starting the enamel work, make sure that the mesh you are going to use to fire on is close at hand and is suitable for the job: once the piece is enamelled and taken off the plasticine and balanced on the palette knife it is not a good idea to have to start looking around for a mesh! Bring the mesh to the piece and not the piece to the mesh.

get carried away on the section being worked on, but always check the enamel that is out of sight at the back of the piece. Enamel will act like a sponge, and while the area being worked on looks fine, the parts already enamelled will have absorbed water while you were working and become wet and fluid, resulting in more enamel on the ring stick than on the ring. Be warned, it is essential to look at everything as it is worked, and not just what is in front of you.

Keep the enamel coats thin, and don't rush the laying: should there be a build-up of the enamel, take the quill and scrape back that area and remove the surplus enamel, and then re-work that section until everything is satisfactory before going on to firing.

When enamelling over a shape and before starting any second or third coats, look over the surface. If it is uneven and patchy, take a fine carborundum stone and stone down those areas a little, then brush them out and fire. This will help balance the colour of the enamel before continuing. However, be aware that stoning up a curved or shaped surface with a hard, rigid carborundum stone can be difficult, and sometimes the enameller needs alternative options to get into those shaped areas. Diagrit strips are more suitable for shapes such as this. Diagrit is a diamond-impregnated, cloth-backed product which has the benefit of being flexible, enabling it to fit into and over curved shapes. It can be bought in 20 × 100mm strips, which are available in four grades, from coarse to very fine.

Using a central screw style of ring stick to hold the piece while enamelling works well, but remember not to tighten the screw too much.

Starting at the 'North Pole' point, begin to lay a first section of enamel.

Lay each section as you go as evenly as you can, and do not move on to the next section until it looks right.

Using the cotton cloth, take out all the water from that first section.

Leaving a slight gap, begin to lay the next section; when this is done, quickly connect the two together.

As before, use the cotton cloth to absorb surplus water.

Continue the same process, working around the ring.

Don't rush: proceed section by section, connecting each one as you go.

Use the cotton cloth to control the water as you lay...

...eventually meeting back up with the section you started at.

Hold the ring stick over the firing mesh, then unscrew the ring stick, letting the ring carefully ease down.

Fire the first coat to an orange-peel finish, then repeat for the second coat, and if needed the third, before stoning down.

GRADING COLOURS

The term 'grading colours' does not describe a technique as such: rather, it is the way an enameller can blend and overlay his enamels to create colour changes and effects, similar to the result that different coloured filters achieve when used in a theatre spotlight. Because the light passes freely through transparent enamel, light is reflected and bounced back from the metal surface itself, especially if that metal surface has been engraved with bright reflective cuts. When this light comes back through the transparent enamel it can be altered by the overlaying and mixing of the enamels, creating a different look.

When enamels are ground you have fine individual grains of glass, but by mixing two ground colours together you will not create a new colour: for example, blue and yellow would not make green enamel, or a red and yellow an orange – it would be more like a screen print, with small, individually coloured grains giving a speckled look. However, if you overlay colours where one colour is first fired down and another colour is overlaid and fired as well, you can create that third colour as the light passes through both colours, like the light passing through those coloured filters in a theatre spotlight.

It is in this respect that the enameller must know his material, how the enamels behave, how they fire and fuse together; this is where he becomes an artist working with his palette of colours. We will take as an example of grading a simple piece with a range of colours from a light blue into mauve into purple, a natural progression where ideally no join or mixing will be seen, just a gentle change and grade as the colours move across the piece.

The choice of colours to use is important, picking shades and density of colour that will work well together; fineness of grain is also important to achieve good results, so make sure the enamels are prepared well. Starting with the lightest, in this case a pale blue, prepare the plate and lay and fire a first coat over the whole surface. Before applying the next colour establish the proportions of the grade, how much of the light colour is to show, and what percentage of the dark is to be seen.

Taking the next choice, the middle colour in the grade, a pale mauve, begin to lay a normal coat over the pale blue, starting where the darkest section will be. Before reaching the point where that colour is to stop, begin to lay the enamel more and more thinly, pulling out the fine grains until they disappear away to nothing; then fire as normal.

Repeat the same process with the last colour, a strong purple: lay this, again starting at the darkest point over the pale mauve, getting thinner and fading out as before, and fire. The piece will now have a layer of pale blue partly overlaid with a faded-out pale mauve, which in turn has been partly overlaid with a faded-out purple; with the light passing through all three colours, a gentle seamless grade going from a pale blue through mauve into purple should have been achieved.

The next stage is to finish up the grade and bring the enamel level before finishing up. Looking from the side, the enamel at one end will be three times as thick as that of the other end. In order to bring up the level without changing the colour grade too much, use flux, a colourless enamel that will fill space without increasing the density of the pale mauve or the purple. Lay the flux starting at the shallow, pale blue end, once again using the same process, starting with a normal thickness of coat, then fading out and up towards the other colours. If desired, more of the light blue and pale mauve can be worked in at the same time to intensify the grade; when this is done, fire.

Lastly add a coat of flux over the whole of the piece, slightly heavier at the pale blue end and getting thinner towards the darker colours. When this is fired, all surfaces should now be level, and the piece can be carefully stoned and given its last fire.

Detail of the abstract floral tazza dish, showing the grading of the enamels.

18ct yellow gold and diamond brooch enamels graded from pale yellow through oranges to rich reds. This piece was specially made for an exhibition at the Goldsmiths' Hall to mark De Vroomen Design's fifty years. RICHARD VALENCIA, COURTESY DE VROOMEN DESIGN LTD

REPAIRING ENAMEL

At some point you will need to repair a piece of enamel, be it one of your own pieces or a piece that has been enamelled some years before by another, maybe unknown enameller. A piece that has come from your own workshop is the lesser problem, as the colours that were used and the way the piece was made will be known. The bigger problem is when you don't know anything about the enamels that were used and their properties, the temperature they fired at, how they behave, even how the piece was made, what solders were used, and if there have been other repairs on the piece before it has reached the workshop.

In cases such as this, the easiest and most practical way is to make a note of the design and match any colours, comparing them to the samples in the workshop's range, then remove all the old enamel work by using hydrofluoric acid and start again, using enamels that are known and trusted. If the damage looks light and the success of a repair looks possible, be mindful that the true condition will not be fully evident until after the first fire. A small chip which has been caused by dropping the piece, for example, could develop cracks which at first were unseen, and these might open up, revealing the true extent of the damage. Before starting, carefully look at what is there; pick off any loose pieces of enamel with an old spitstick, a useful tool to have on the bench at times like this.

If a piece has chipped off altogether and there is a sudden step down in the enamel, use a fine carborundum stone to ease the step down so that when new enamel is applied there will not be a sudden change from the old colour to the new. If all looks fairly sound, brush it out well with the black bristle brush under running water, removing all dirt and the remnants of any old enamel, and give the piece a light fire.

If the chip was down to the metal base, this must be covered with a thin coat of enamel to avoid the metal oxidizing; then fire the piece lightly. More damage may become evident, in which case follow the same procedure as above, again until eventually, when the piece is fired, it looks clean and any damage has gone.

Continue by adding more thin layers, overlapping them and blending them in with the existing enamel, and finish as normal.

Dealing with Diamonds in a Piece to be Repaired

Diamonds are the only stone that can be considered safe to put through the kiln, and even then, care must be taken. If the stone is large and of good quality it would be wise to have the piece unset before attempting the repair, as when putting diamonds through the kiln there is a chance of what is known as *burning* happening. It is thought that a cool draught reaching the stone as it comes out of the heat can discolour or dull the stone, and the only option to correct this is to unset and re-polish the stones; however, with most small stones this is impractical, making the diamonds unusable.

Before starting any work and before any firing takes place, to help prevent damage, take a borax dish and cone, add a small amount of water and mix it into a creamy paste; then paint this over the diamond, front and back, and any area that is likely to become exposed to heat. Let this dry out well before enamelling. The borax will act as a barrier as you fire, and hopefully will protect the diamond from any draught. Also, when you take the piece out of the kiln, cover it with an upturned Pyrex bowl or a tin.

This is as much as can be done, and it is not 100 per cent foolproof, but in most cases it will work. Nevertheless, it is wise to advise any client before starting a repair with diamonds that it is at their own risk, and if there is concern, then the diamonds must be removed – the enameller can't take the blame for everything!

To sum up, when repairing any piece, pay close attention the first time the piece is fired, observing constantly until it can be established that all is well in the kiln. As mentioned above, often the history of a piece is unknown, and many antique pieces from the past were constructed using lead solder after the enamelling process – so beware!

PROBLEM SOLVING

When enamel work is going wrong and problems arise it will be necessary to try and work out why and how to rectify this. Most problems can be traced back through the process, so first look at the metal and its cleaning and preparation, and ask yourself if enough was done? Were the enamels ground enough, washed well enough, and fired to the right point and not overfired? Look at the amount of enamel applied at each coat: were the layers too thick? When brushing out the piece after its last stone and finishing, were there white marks left on the surface where it was touched by fingers?

At some point the offending action will become clear, and hopefully it can be corrected, or at worse the piece may have to be restarted – but at least it will be understood why it went wrong.

The process of developing any skill involves learning from mistakes. It has been mentioned before in this book that when enamelling, every process has to be given attention, and any one of the processes not carried out correctly will have an effect on the piece; this may be not so obvious as to warrant starting again, but it will mean the results are not what they could or should be. Enamelling is not a science, it is an art, and problems will always arise; what is done on one day with fantastic results, on the next with the same process can result in a problem – but don't get downhearted, it happens to us all!

CHAPTER 9

Kilns and Firing

Enamellers don't require much equipment or machinery: the kiln is our life source, our workhorse, the everyday and hopefully reliable piece of kit that makes our job possible. I don't know who thought of fusing glass on to metal – I expect it was discovered by mistake, as a lot of things are, but I doubt if it was much different from the way we work today. There are electric and gas kilns available with sophisticated, computerized temperature controls – but despite all these benefits it still comes down to a chamber with surrounding heat, creating a temperature which allows us to do what we do: fuse glass to metal.

Early enamellers would still have had a chamber-style furnace. A heat source would have been created from burning wood or peat, packed around the outer walls, with the firing chamber space probably sealed. The work inside would have been left for a pre-established length of time to fire. We can never know exactly how they worked, but there are enough examples in museums to make sense of their knowledge and techniques.

Over the years kilns and kiln technology have developed, coke-fired kilns came in, later giving way to gas and electric kilns. Working became more controlled and cleaner – but in essence we are performing the same tasks as our predecessors did hundreds of years earlier.

Tools and equipment for use during firing.

The kilns I have used in my workshops have all been electric, but I do recollect one of my first workshop visits with Dad on a Saturday where there was a gas kiln. My impression as a young boy was that there were lots of pipes and tubes, and when a taper was placed inside to light it, there was a loud whoosh as the gas ignited, and it felt as if it could blow your eyebrows off!

The first firing of the base trumpet section of the Dunwich dish.

Use a kiln size suitable for the size of piece to be enamelled. This small Paragon kiln has a chamber size of 190mm wide, 140mm high and 190mm deep, and works well for jewellery and small objects.

The larger Carbolite kiln has a chamber size of 210mm wide, 210mm high and 310mm deep, and is used when working on larger pieces.

WHAT IS IMPORTANT IN A KILN?

So what is important in a kiln, and what should you look for when buying one? The size of the chamber will be important, and it should be appropriate to the work it is required for. If it is only going to be used for enamelling jewellery, then a kiln 300mm square isn't needed; but if objects and larger pieces are likely to be enamelled, then that extra size will be required. To fire up a large kiln just to fire something brooch sized is a waste of energy, so my suggestion is to purchase a kiln appropriate to the size of pieces that are going to be made in the workshop, and if need be have kilns with varying chamber sizes to cover all aspects of work. I have three kilns in my workshop with small, medium and large chamber sizes.

ELECTRIC OR GAS?

Enamellers will have different views on whether to buy gas or electric. Do gas kilns bring more oxygen into the flame, giving a better result to some colours, or do other colours work better in electric kilns? Invariably it will be a personal choice, but whatever you decide to buy, irrespective of the pros and cons of one colour working better with gas or another working better with electric, that will be your kiln and you will have to accept its good and bad points.

Good insulation in a kiln is important; you don't want half the heat disappearing out through the kiln's body. An accurate temperature control is also a big consideration. The ability of your kiln to hold and maintain your desired working temperature is a must. Laying enamel over a complicated design could take several hours, and the last thing you need when you open the kiln door to fire is to see the inside glowing white with heat, or worse, a colder, dull red. To have your kiln at a constant temperature and always ready to fire is a bonus. Lastly it is important that your kiln has the ability to return quickly to your desired working temperature.

Ask practising enamellers what kilns they use, and search out their recommendations – this will at least be a good point to start from. Cost may be a consideration too, but try and buy the best you can: breaking down that initial cost over the kiln's life makes the outlay, although high at first, very economical.

FIRING

Please remember that what I am writing relates to *my* working methods. Every enameller will have their own ideas, their own specific way of working. I run my kiln at 1,000°C (1,832°F) to ensure a quick fire and a rapid build-up of heat, and this helps produce brightness and life in my work. On average, enamels fire at around 750–800°C (1,414–1,472°F) so why the extra 200° (392°F)? Take the test yourself; set your kiln at 750°/800° (1,414–1,472°F) and notice how far your kiln temperature will drop during a normal firing – up to 200°C (392°F) on average can be lost. Just opening the door will lose heat; the mesh you are firing on will absorb more heat and the piece itself more again. Your kiln temperature will drop well below the enamel firing temperature, and heat will then have to build back up, extending and dragging on the firing time, with the end result of a duller look.

You may not even have noticed this, but try firing at the higher temperature. As a young apprentice when we were firing reds, the first fire was always done on a gas blow torch with the air pressure coming from a set of old leather foot bellows, and this ensured a rapid fire, even quicker than the kiln. With the coming of town gas into London, our bellows were taken away by the Gas Board for health and safety reasons! But I

Silver 'fish' dish. This piece was photo-etched flat and then formed up into a shallow plate, trimmed up, carved, engraved and enamelled. It sits on a heavy wire base with three cast silver frog supporters. Designed, engraved and enamelled by Phil Barnes. 170mm diameter.
PRIVATE COLLECTION

still try and achieve that first rapid fire. As long as you get that first coat looking good it will continue to look good throughout.

Let's touch on one thing that is often said, which is 'you can't get a good red on silver unless you lay it over flux'. Well no, I don't believe that to be true, and as long as you clean your silver correctly, remove all fire stain as we have previously mentioned in Chapter 6 and fire as I have explained, you will achieve a good red.

HOW LONG TO FIRE AND WHAT TO LOOK FOR

If you have experience of soldering, relate that process to firing your enamels. You don't just put a flame on the piece you are soldering and gaze out of the window: you look, watching for signs, and when the solder has reached the right temperature and begins to flow, you know when to remove your flame. Too soon and the solder won't flow, too late and the solder starts to burn, and firing enamel is similar.

Even before you start enamelling your piece, consider the way it will fire: what support will be needed, how will the piece heat up, will you need to turn the piece around to gain an even heat during firing? If one end of the piece is made of thinner material, should you consider putting that end towards the front of the kiln, or in extreme cases put a thin piece of firebrick under that area to slow down and balance out the heating-up process? On a large piece I will have a dummy run to see what it will be like getting the piece in and out of the kiln, and it is best to do that before you start to lay your enamel, not leave it until you have a piece all enamelled and ready to fire.

Every time a piece is fired there is the capacity to ruin the work: this may sound dramatic, but if the piece in the kiln is not given 100 per cent concentration, then the worst must be expected! Standard silver has a melting point of around 890°C (1,680°F) and gold 900°C (1,652°F), so you can see you have more than enough heat to melt the piece.

Be aware all the time of what is going on in the kiln, and be ready to act when the right point of firing is reached. Firing in itself is a very quick process – we are not firing a piece of pottery that needs the temperature to be built up slowly and then left overnight to cool down, we are talking about a quick firing, as quick as a minute for a small piece or up to ten minutes or more for a larger object.

THE FIRING PROCESS

First introduce the piece to the heat slowly. During enamelling most of the water is absorbed out of the enamel using a clean cotton cloth. There will be some moisture left: the bigger the area that has been enamelled, the more moisture the enamel will hold. I don't sit my work on top of the kiln to dry out as some enamellers do, as I believe this is not necessary – it leaves your piece open to the atmosphere and any dirt and dust floating around the workshop.

On opening the kiln door I slowly introduce the piece to the heat – I like to think of it as saying 'hello' to the kiln: with a kiln set at 1,000°C (1,832°F) any moisture remaining will very soon evaporate. Observation is the key thing in firing: there is no need to stare constantly into the kiln, just a quick peek around the kiln door will be more than enough to judge which point the firing process is at.

Silver 'blue leaves' vase. Engraved and enamelled, with a second level of bright cut leaves engraved to give more depth after enamelling. Designed, engraved and enamelled by Phil Barnes. 115mm high, 60mm at its widest point. PRIVATE COLLECTION

THE SIGNS TO LOOK FOR

First you will notice the enamel will darken, and this will happen whatever your enamel – this is difficult to see if it is a dark shade to start with, but you will still see a change. As the piece heats up, that dark look will begin to lighten, and this is the first sign that the enamel is beginning to fire; also you may notice that any texture engraved beneath the enamel starts to become visible. This stage we would describe as 'sugar', as the enamel takes on the appearance of sugar grains.

By all means, if you are uncertain as to what is happening in the kiln, remove the piece briefly and have a

Firing on a section of firebrick will help maintain a flat finish to the piece.

closer look, then return it to the kiln – but remember, it doesn't matter how quickly this is done, the kiln will lose temperature, therefore increasing the firing time.

From the sugar look of the enamel, the next point to look for is a surface like orange peel – some smooth areas, but also some small bumps and depressions (sinks). The enamel at this point is fired, but we want to go just past that stage until those bumps and sinks have become more regular, showing a more uniform appearance over the entire surface. On the first coat of enamel it is not necessary to fire the piece fully, by which I mean to a smooth, level surface – in fact if we did, the chances of causing some damage to the enamel would be great, for instance, burning it around the edges.

Where the enamel has been laid a little thin it could be found that it has burnt out altogether, leaving silver patches showing through, something that we hadn't wanted to happen. However, as the enamelling process progresses and we apply coat on coat, subsequent fires will increase in time, but the thicker enamel layers are more able to cope with the higher temperatures without showing signs of damage. The last fire is always the longest and hottest, to achieve that smooth, final finish.

Kiln Health and Safety

The first thing to say when working with a kiln is that it is very, very hot! An obvious remark I know, but have respect for that heat. It isn't just the inside of the kiln that is hot: the casing of the kiln, the meshes that are used, the fork or tongs used during firing – all these will hold heat for some time. The use of gloves during firing is encouraged. With time, handling hot things becomes second nature, and the bright orange of the kiln will soon cease to cause anxiety – but this is no reason to lose respect for what can happen. Looking into the kiln has been a concern for some people: does it dry out your eyes, or will it cause cataracts in later years? When I refer to looking into the kiln, I am not talking about staring wide-eyed into 1,000°C (1,832°F): all that is required is the occasional peek through the crack of a slightly opened kiln door. There are protective glasses available to use if you wish.

Firing is an immediate process, the same as the soldering of a piece during making would be.

Like soldering, the firing of enamel needs your full attention.

A quick look into the chamber is enough to check how things are progressing.

It can be that one side of the kiln may be hotter than the other, or the piece you are firing is an unbalanced shape.

It is good practice to take the piece out half way through and turn the mesh, then put it back in the kiln; this gives a more even heat distribution.

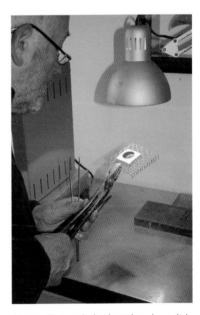

Above all, watch, look at the piece. It is better to know what is going on in the kiln than not – you can always put the piece back in and continue firing.

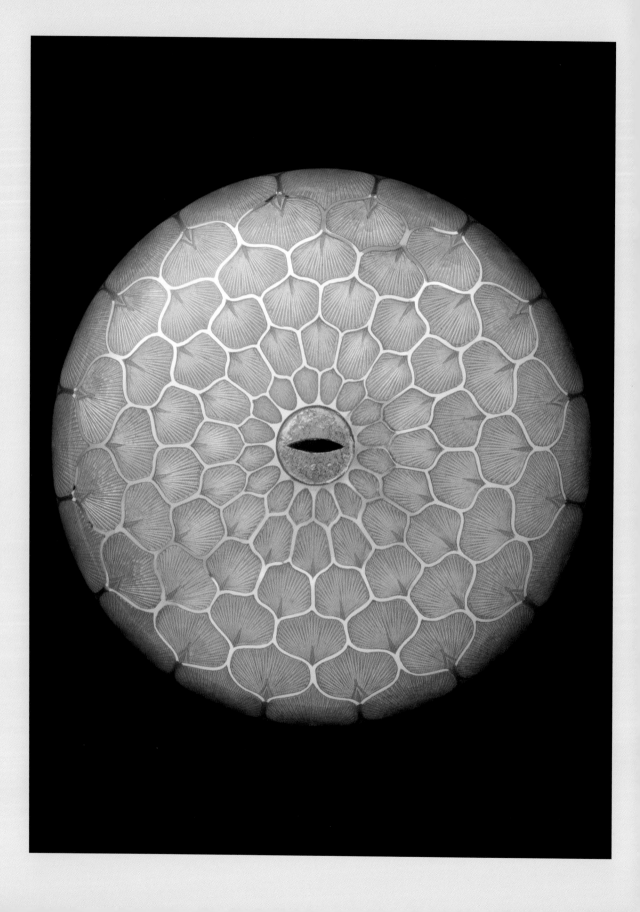

CHAPTER 10

Polishing and Finishing

When the piece has had its last fire and is pickled, some enamellers would leave it there, but this is not the end of the process: a good piece of enamelling is defined by the way it is finished. Not all enamels fire with a smooth, flat finish: most will have a wave or a ripple to the surface, and because of the retraction of the enamel at each fire, the surface will have shrunk slightly and will be lower than the metal edges of the cells. Bringing up the surface and levelling the enamel with the metal around it defines a well finished piece. This process of polishing the enamel is described as lapping.

EQUIPMENT AND MATERIALS

Regarding the equipment and materials needed for polishing, the main piece of equipment to achieve a good finish is the polishing motor itself. An average speed for a normal polishing motor for jewellery or silverwork is around 2,500 to 2,800rpm, but for enamels a much slower speed is required, around 1,100 to 1,250rpm. The motor also needs to be mounted and raised up to allow for easy access when working. Ideally the polishing motor should be an enclosed unit, as the lapping process uses water, so for safety the introduction of foot-controlled on/off power switches will save wet hands getting near the electrical supply.

The compound used to polish is a fine pumice powder with a grade of 240 mesh; this is mixed with water to form a double cream consistency, and held in a plastic tray sitting below the wheel. The aim of lapping is to take the silver and enamel down until all surfaces look and feel as one. The 240 mesh pumice powder will have enough bite to achieve this and create the final finish, yet still keep a shine on the enamel surface.

The polishing wheels used are made of hard felt and come in varying sizes and widths, and are generally flat. It is good to have a range of wheel sizes to cover all aspects of work. A felt wheel will wear down with use, but never throw anything away, because as a wheel loses its flat surface it develops a gentle curve, and this then becomes ideal for polishing shaped pieces; just replace the worn wheel with a fresh flat wheel to take on those flat surfaces, and keep the curve for curves. As this process continues and the curves become more pronounced, the wheels can all be moved down a step – in time you will have a collection of shapes and sizes to fit all pieces. The largest wheel I use is 200mm diam-

Snake box in vivid greens and acid yellows. Designed, engraved and enamelled with graded colours by Phil Barnes. 70mm diameter. PRIVATE COLLECTION

The enameller's polishing motor: this motor has an RPM of 1,420 and is raised up on blocks to allow for the polishing wheels to fit underneath. The tray below the spindle holds a mix of pumice powder and water.

Wheels to lap the enamels are made of hard felt and come in different sizes; also black brush wheels are used for the final finish.

eter and the smallest is 50mm, and there is every shape and size in between.

Calico mops and bristle brush wheels are also used, not for lapping but for gentle polishing over the surface when the lapping is completed. These are still used with the pumice and water mix, and charged in the same way as the felt wheels; they help give both the metal and enamel their final shine. One of the hardest pieces to lap and to achieve that mirror-like surface is a large flat piece. Very few pieces are actually dead flat, even if they are supposed to be, so make allowances for this as the work goes along, and don't just clamp the piece on to a flat wheel and expect a perfect result – it needs constant watching as it is worked, altering the pressure and the amount of pumice used, making adjustments as and where needed.

When it is necessary to achieve this high finish you could use a boxwood wheel for the final stage. Boxwood is a slow-growing shrub and produces a dense, unusually stable wood; in the past it was used for making rulers and scientific instruments. Wheels made from boxwood have a harder working surface, and can be used to give the final finish to the piece. However, boxwood wheels are not easy to come by now: they are not offered by general tool suppliers, but if one can be found it is worth having just for those special flat pieces.

The action of lapping is to use the side of the felt wheel, charging the surface with the pumice and water mix as it is worked. A new wheel will absorb a lot of water to begin with, and it is a good idea to let it soak in water for an hour or so to bring it to a working condition; but over time the wheels will become embedded with the pumice and this absorption of water will stop. Keep the wheel wet, but try not to flood the surface with too much water; it is the pumice that will do the work, not the water, so aim for a balanced, creamy pumice and water mix.

It is important to keep the piece moving when lapping: if it remains still, fixed in one place, drag marks will be created, lines going in the direction of the wheel, and this will happen even with the comparatively slow speed of the motor. This is why a slower speed is needed: using a motor with an rpm of 2,800 would result in the pumice tearing into both the enamel and the metal around it, causing damage to the surface.

Keep up a gentle rhythm, moving the piece back and forth, changing direction over the surface of the wheel. You will need to exert some pressure, but not

When lapping, the side of the wheel is used; this is charged up with a creamy water and pumice mix.

A slight pressure is applied and a constant movement is needed as the pumice polishes, taking the metal and the enamel down to one level.

Polishing is a task that needs time – rushing and pushing too hard can put drags into the enamel if you are not careful, so stop frequently and look closely at the surface to establish what needs to be done.

too much: listen to the sound of the motor, start lightly and begin to increase pressure, and as you do so the sound of the motor will become slightly deeper – but press too hard, and the sound will change again, and you will notice that the wheel slows down. The middle range of pressure is what is needed.

As the wheel begins to dry, recharge with the pumice and water; use old rags for this purpose, rolled up into a ball and held in the hand – the pumice and water will be absorbed easily into the cotton, and it will fit comfortably into the palm of the hand. It is worth remembering that prior to the last fire of a piece it may have been necessary to add a few odd dots of enamel to bring small sinks up to level; however, this will not mean having to stone and re-fire, because the pumice, along with the felt wheel, can easily polish down any small bumps like that and still keep a good shiny surface. Likewise if a piece gets scratched, as it sometimes can during setting or fitting up, then that can be polished out, saving the problem of having to go through the kiln again.

The enameller's polishing room is quite a dirty place, with dried out pumice and unused polishing wheels and brushes on the bench, and it is a good idea if possible to have a separate area for lapping or polishing away from the general workshop – and especially away from any area used for finishing any highly polished work. If any pumice gets into the mops and felts used for that, it would have disastrous results.

FINAL FINISHING OF THE METAL

The pumice will have done two things: it will have polished the enamel, and also the surrounding metal surface, removing marks and scratches caused during stoning down – and in the case of silver, it will have removed most of the fire stain left in the surface. Using a standard jewellery polishing motor with a speed of 2,800rpm is fine to finish the metal; the surface achieved with the pumice should allow you to go directly to rouge or any fine polishing compound. Rouge does not have the bite of pumice and will cause your enamels no harm, though be aware that if a coarser compound is chosen, Tripoli for example, this could cause some problems if worked too hard, and surfaces may be affected, especially the soft enamels.

The enameller's polishing room is a dirty place with dried pumice clinging to every surface. This area should be kept apart from any place used for final high speed polishing of the metal.

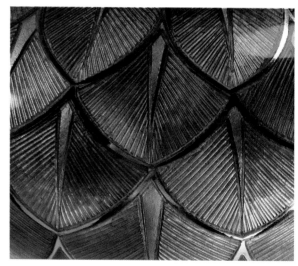

The aim of polishing is to bring both the enamel and silver surfaces down to one level, giving that smooth and perfect finish.

When it comes to the final cleaning up of the piece, the use of an ultrasonic unit should work well, but always use hot, not boiling water, and do not leave the piece in the ultrasonic for any longer than is necessary. Gilding and gold plating a piece is generally successful, but there are certain things to ask the plater to do to ensure that success. When preparing the piece for plating, do not place the contact wires across the enamel surface, and turn down the current in the plating plant slightly. The pigments in enamels are metal oxides, and certain enamels, especially some older reds and purples for example, can be gold based, so the process of gold plating can unsettle those colours and result in cracking. Bearing in mind these precautions should help alleviate this problem.

Health and Safety with Polishing Motors

There are basic rules when working with any machinery, especially with polishing motors. Tie back any long hair, don't wear loose clothing, take off any rings or bracelets, and take off neck chains. Wear goggles, but never gloves of any kind. When polishing with pumice and water, keep wet hands away from any direct power source. Be aware how abrasive pumice can be: you may not feel as if anything is happening, but a finger resting against a felt wheel as you work will soon wear through! Above all, concentration and attention to the task in hand is important.

Silver snake box in blue greys. Designed, engraved and enamelled with graded colours with a moonstone top by Phil Barnes. 70mm in diameter. PRIVATE COLLECTION

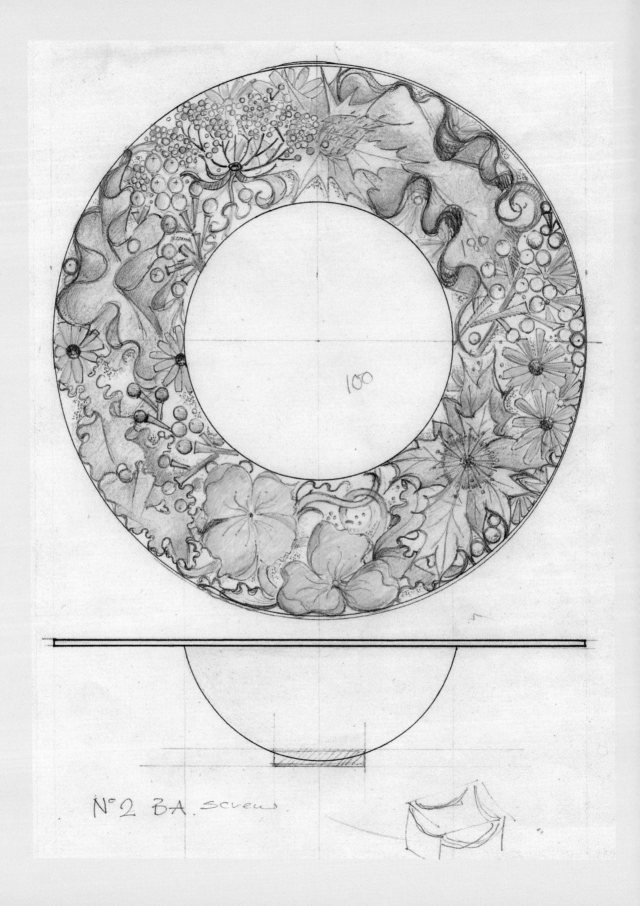

100

190

N°2 BA. Screw.

Useful Information

Included in this chapter are lists and names of suppliers of materials that are used in my workshop, also some useful contacts of organizations that may help if this book has inspired you to take up engraving and enamelling.

All the images shown in this book, apart from the historical ones, are of work carried out in my workshop; most are of pieces designed, made, engraved and enamelled by me, while there are also a few show pieces where I have engraved and enamelled with and for other jewellers and goldsmiths – I have included below their website details to show further examples of their work.

Elizabeth Gage Ltd
www.elizabeth-gage.com

De Vroomen Design Ltd
www.devroomen.co.uk

Roger Doyle Ltd
www.rogerdoyle.co.uk

Henn of London
www.hennoflondon.co.uk

The original drawing for the design of the top section of the Dunwich Bowl.

Suppliers of Tools

H. S. Walsh
General jewellery tools and engraving equipment.
www.hswalsh.com

Sutton Tools/Betts
General jewellery tools and engraving equipment.
UK agent for GRS systems.
www.bettsmetalsales.com

Cookson Precious Metals
General tool suppliers and bullion dealers.
www.cooksongold.com

Suppliers of Enamels

Milton Bridge Ceramic Colours Ltd
Makers of Schauer, Latham, Milton Bridge
and 263 series enamels. (Latham enamels were
originally Wenger Ltd, 263 Series were originally
Blythe colours.)
www.milton-bridge.co.uk

Emaux Soyer
Makers and suppliers of Soyer enamels.
www.emaux-soyer.com

Vitrum Signum
General enamelling supplies, also agent for Blythe,
Ninomiya, British Professional, Milton Bridge,
Schauer and Soyer enamels.
www.vitrumsignum.com

Precious Metal Suppliers

Cookson Precious Metals
Silver and gold bullion, sheet, wire, tubing, chain etc.
www.cooksongold.com

Metalor
Precious metals and bullion.
www.metalor.com

Suppliers of Acid

R & L Slaughter Ltd
www.slaughter.co.uk

H. S. Walsh
www.hswalsh.com

The Aslan pin. The lion's head is a carved bi-coloured tourmaline with a bold pattern, engraved and enamelled in opaque black enamel. Enamelled for Elizabeth Gage.

Silver Spinning

Mr Stefan Coe
01276 857799

Metal Polishing and Finishing

Elliot & Fitzpatrick
www.elliot-fitzpatrick.com

Kiln Suppliers

Paragon kilns
www.paragonweb.com

Carbolite
www.carbolite-gero.com

Art Suppliers and Gold Foils

Stuart Stevenson
www.stuartstevenson.co.uk

Engine Turning

Steve Keen
01733 203600

Safety Data Sheets

Any chemical supplier will produce their own safety data sheets. Below are three companies as a starting point for you to research.

VWR Chemicals
www.u.k.vwr.com

Fisher Scientific
www.fishersci.com

Triachem
www.triachem.com

Organizations

The British Society of Enamellers
www.enamellers.org

Guild of Enamellers
www.guildofenamellers.org

The Hand Engravers Association of Great Britain
www.handengravers.co.uk

Close-up showing detail of an engraved and enamelled box top.

A Guide to Estimating Temperatures in Relation to Various Metals

Temperatures given in °C

232	Tin melts
419	Zinc melts
500–600	Faint red glow
650–700	Dull red
800	Cherry red
893	Standard silver melts
900	Bright red
961	Fine silver melts
1,000	Very bright red, verging into yellow
1,063	Fine gold melts
1,280	White heat
1,773	Platinum melts

Temperature Conversion Table

°C	°F
0	32
25	77
50	122
100	212
200	392
300	572
400	752
500	932
600	1,112
700	1,292
800	1,472
900	1,652
1,000	1,832

Inside a kiln at 1,000°C.

Melting Points of Solders

Cookson Precious Metals Ltd

Silver Solders

Extra easy	665–710°C
Easy	705–725°C
Medium	720–765°C
Hard	745–780°C
Enamelling	730–800°C

Gold Solders

Easy	700–715°C
Medium	730–765°C
Hard	790–830°C

18ct yellow gold and diamond picture frame. Engraved and enamelled
for Roger Doyle Ltd. 140mm high, 125mm wide.

Glossary of Terms

architects drafting film   A plastic version of tracing paper. More resilient to use.

bassetaille   An enamelling technique where a low relief design is carved beneath the enamelled surface, creating a monotone result.

blue   A term relating to a softened steel, back end of a graver or the end of a file.

borax   A silica that comes as a dish and cone, and is used as a flux when soldering or for use when firing diamonds.

boxwood   A tightly grained hardwood.

Britannia   .950 grade of silver.

calamus   The central stem of a quill.

calico   A multi-layered polishing mop.

carborundum   Carborundum is a trademark name for a synthetic silicon carbide that has been produced since 1893. It is a man-made, very hard material with the particles of silicon carbide being bonded together. These can be purchased in many shapes – square, triangular, even round – and come in varying coarseness of cut.

champlevé   An enamel technique where a cell is created by engraving, etching or stamping to which enamel is then applied.

chenier   Small silver tubing.

clear fire   A gum which can be used with enamel.

cloisonné   Where the cells of a design in a piece of enamelling are formed by applied wires and then filled with enamel.

counter enamel   Enamel applied to the underside of a piece to help counter stress, often used with thinner material or with finer grades of material to help combat cracking and distortion in the piece.

Diagrit   Diagrit is a diamond-impregnated, cloth-backed product which has the benefit of being flexible, enabling it to fit into and over curved shapes. It can be bought in strips 20 × 100mm and is available in four grades from coarse to very fine.

engine turning   A hand-driven machine that creates an accurate, repeated, single line cut pattern.

firestain   The build-up of copper oxide on the surface of silver when annealing or soldering.

18ct yellow gold diamond and tourmaline necklace.
Enamelled for Henn of London.

GRS engraving system   An air-powered engraving system.

guilloche   An engine-turned pattern engraved into the surface under enamel producing high reflection.

half round   An engraving tool with a round bottom to the tool. Used for outlining and texturing under enamel.

HSS tools   High Speed Steel engraving tools have a yellow-ended tang and are made of tougher steel.

hydrofluoric acid   Used for the removal of enamel.

lapping   The use of pumice powder on felt wheels to polish the enamel surface.

Micro-Mesh   Fine, rubber-backed polishing material ideal for the backs of engraving tools.

nitric acid   Used for the cleaning of standard silver to remove firestain.

opaque   Dense solid enamels.

optivisor   Magnifying headband.

pestle and mortar   Used for grinding enamels.

pickle   Mixture of sulphuric acid and water. Ten parts water to one part acid used for the cleaning of golds and the bringing back of colour to the metal after heating.

plasticine   A clay-like modelling material Trademark of Flair Leisure Products plc.

pliqué a jour   An enamelling technique used in jewellery which has the effect of miniature stained-glass windows.

porosity   Found in castings, small air pockets within the metal.

pumice powder   Used for the lapping and polishing of enamel. 240 mesh is mixed with water to a creamy consistency for use on felt wheels.

purified water   Treated water used to wash enamels after grinding.

Pyrex   A trade name for heat-resistant glass.

quill   A cut-down feather used for the application of enamels.

rpm   Revolutions per minute.

sandbags   Round leather discs sewn together and filled with sand. Used for working on and raising up work when engraving.

scorper   Another name for a flat engraving tool. Flat scorper.

SDS   Safety data sheets.

sellotape   Clear, sticky-backed tape.

setters wax   A sealing wax-type substance used for the mounting up of work while engraving.

spitstick   An engraving tool used for trimming edges and corners in champlevé.

sprue   The feeder point for metal in a casting pattern.

standard   .925 grade of silver.

tang   Softer back end of a graver or file, usually blued.

Thermoloc   A method of holding work; this material goes from a solid state to soft and back again by the application of heat, either by hot water or a hot air gun and then cooling in cold water.

translucent   Opal enamels, semi-transparent.

transparent   Completely clear enamels.

vacuum casting   A casting process where oxygen is absent, cutting out firestain.

vane   Feather part of a quill.

Index

'Folded materials' lidded beaker with saucer; designed, engraved and enamelled by Phil Barnes. Beaker 105mm high and 64mm at the widest point, with the saucer at 145mm diameter. PRIVATE COLLECTION

Related Titles from Crowood

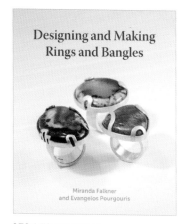

978 1 78500 318 9

978 1 78500 232 8

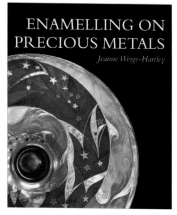

978 1 84797 205 7

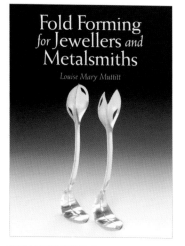

978 1 78500 272 4

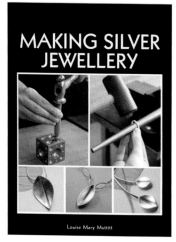

978 1 84797 683 3

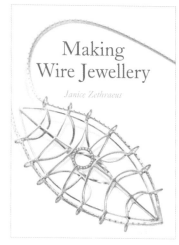

978 1 78500 165

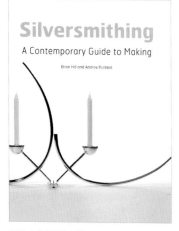

978 1 84797 615 4

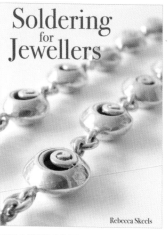

978 1 78500 247 8

978 1 84797 413 6